MASTERING SQL SERVER

SERVER

Become a Pro in Database Administration and Query Optimization

THOMPSON CARTER

TABLE OF CONTENTS

INTRODUCTION

Introduction to Mastering SQL Server

Relational databases have been at the heart of business applications for decades, and SQL Server is one of the most powerful tools in this arena. Whether you're managing a small business database or architecting an enterprise-level data system, **SQL Server provides the robustness, scalability, and flexibility** needed for modern applications. But despite its popularity, getting the most out of SQL Server requires more than just a basic understanding of SQL. It requires hands-on knowledge of SQL Server's unique tools, best practices, and tuning techniques.

Why SQL Server?

Microsoft SQL Server has established itself as a leading choice for businesses, ranging from startups to global enterprises. Its strength lies in its reliability, ease of use, and advanced features that allow data professionals to efficiently store, retrieve, and manipulate data. SQL Server isn't just a database; it's a comprehensive platform that supports complex data solutions, including real-time analytics, machine learning integrations, and reporting services.

SQL Server also includes capabilities that enhance data security and integrity, allowing businesses to manage user permissions, encrypt sensitive information, and recover data quickly in case of emergencies. As organizations grow increasingly data-driven, these features make SQL Server a critical skill set for IT professionals.

Who This Book is For

This book is crafted for **developers, database administrators, data analysts, and IT professionals** who want to master SQL Server in a practical, real-world context. It assumes a basic familiarity with relational databases and SQL but doesn't require prior expertise in SQL Server. Our focus is on hands-on experience, so readers will find step-by-step examples, clear explanations, and tips that can be applied immediately in any work environment.

What You'll Learn

Throughout this book, you'll develop skills that go beyond simple querying. We'll explore essential SQL Server features and real-world scenarios, ensuring you have the foundational skills to:

1. **Build and manage SQL Server databases** from the ground up.
2. **Optimize query performance** with indexing strategies and advanced query techniques.
3. **Automate tasks** with stored procedures, triggers, and custom functions.
4. **Enhance data security and integrity** with SQL Server's advanced security tools.

5. **Set up and manage backup and recovery solutions** to protect valuable data.

6. **Analyze and visualize data** with SQL Server Reporting Services (SSRS) and other integration tools.

7. **Monitor and tune the server** to handle even the heaviest workloads.

8. **Migrate and upgrade SQL Server environments**, ensuring minimal downtime and data loss.

By the end of the book, you'll have a toolkit of practical SQL Server knowledge, with each chapter building your skillset through direct, no-jargon explanations and examples.

How to Use This Book

Each chapter is designed to stand on its own, allowing you to explore topics independently or sequentially, depending on your current needs or skill level. Real-world examples and exercises at the end of each chapter help reinforce the material, so you can apply what you've learned directly to your SQL Server environment.

CHAPTER 1: INTRODUCTION TO SQL SERVER

Overview of SQL Server

Microsoft SQL Server is a relational database management system (RDBMS) developed by Microsoft, known for its stability, performance, and integration capabilities within the Microsoft ecosystem. SQL Server is designed to store, retrieve, and manage data for a variety of applications, ranging from small web applications to large-scale enterprise solutions. As a robust platform, it enables data professionals to perform advanced operations, such as data analysis, business intelligence, and even machine learning, all within a single ecosystem.

The Role of SQL in SQL Server

Structured Query Language, or SQL, is the core language used to communicate with SQL Server. SQL enables users to create and modify database structures, insert and update data, and query the database to retrieve specific information. SQL Server builds upon standard SQL with additional capabilities and proprietary features, such as Transact-SQL (T-SQL), Microsoft's proprietary extension to SQL that offers more control and functionality.

T-SQL introduces features like error handling, control-of-flow statements, and support for complex business logic within the database. Mastering T-SQL is crucial for effectively using SQL

Server, as it allows for more powerful and efficient data manipulation.

SQL Server Editions and Versions

SQL Server is available in several editions, each designed to cater to different types of users and workloads. These editions include:

1. **SQL Server Express**: A free version ideal for small applications, development, and testing. It has limitations on database size and hardware usage but provides a cost-effective solution for small-scale projects.

2. **SQL Server Standard**: Designed for small to medium-sized businesses, this edition supports most SQL Server features with moderate scalability and performance options.

3. **SQL Server Enterprise**: The most powerful edition, suitable for large organizations and mission-critical applications, offering advanced features such as high availability, advanced security, and support for larger workloads.

4. **SQL Server Developer**: A free edition with the same features as the Enterprise version, intended for development and testing purposes rather than production environments.

Microsoft regularly releases updates to SQL Server, each with new features, enhancements, and performance improvements. Staying current with these updates can be vital for leveraging new tools and maintaining compatibility with modern systems.

SQL Server Architecture

Understanding SQL Server's architecture is essential to using the platform effectively. SQL Server's architecture includes several core components:

- **Database Engine**: The core service that processes queries, stores data, and manages database objects.
- **SQL Server Agent**: A job scheduler that automates routine tasks such as backups and maintenance.
- **SQL Server Management Studio (SSMS)**: A graphical interface for managing SQL Server instances and performing database administration tasks.
- **SQL Server Integration Services (SSIS)**: A tool for data integration and workflow automation, useful for ETL (Extract, Transform, Load) processes.
- **SQL Server Reporting Services (SSRS)**: A reporting tool for creating, managing, and delivering reports.
- **SQL Server Analysis Services (SSAS)**: A tool for data analysis and building complex analytical models.

Each of these components plays a unique role, allowing SQL Server to support a wide range of data management and business intelligence requirements.

SQL Server Use Cases

SQL Server is versatile and widely used across industries. Common use cases include:

1. **Transactional Databases**: SQL Server is widely used to support applications that handle real-time transactions, such as e-commerce websites and point-of-sale systems.

2. **Data Warehousing**: SQL Server provides tools for aggregating and analyzing large datasets, making it ideal for business intelligence and data warehousing projects.

3. **Business Intelligence (BI)**: With SSRS, SSIS, and SSAS, SQL Server supports end-to-end BI solutions, allowing organizations to collect, process, and analyze data for informed decision-making.

4. **Web Applications**: SQL Server can store and manage the backend data for web applications, providing robust security, transaction support, and scalability.

5. **Integration with Microsoft Ecosystem**: SQL Server integrates seamlessly with other Microsoft products, such as Azure, Power BI, and SharePoint, providing additional flexibility for Microsoft-centric environments.

Benefits of SQL Server

SQL Server offers several advantages that make it an attractive choice for businesses:

- **Performance and Scalability**: SQL Server can handle both small databases and large-scale applications with millions of transactions per second.

- **Security**: With features like Transparent Data Encryption (TDE), Always Encrypted, and Row-Level Security, SQL Server provides robust protection for sensitive data.

- **High Availability**: Features like Always On Availability Groups and Failover Clustering provide SQL Server with strong options for data redundancy and uptime.

- **Data Integration and Reporting**: Built-in tools like SSIS and SSRS make it easier to work with data from multiple sources and generate reports.

- **Cloud Support**: SQL Server can be deployed on-premises, in the cloud (using Microsoft Azure), or in a hybrid environment, providing flexibility to fit various deployment needs.

The Importance of Mastering SQL Server

Mastering SQL Server can significantly enhance one's ability to work with data-driven applications and make informed decisions. As data continues to be a key driver of business innovation, SQL Server skills are highly valued in roles such as database administrators, developers, data analysts, and business intelligence professionals. In this book, we'll explore each feature of SQL Server in depth, providing practical examples and real-world applications to help you build a solid foundation.

Conclusion

SQL Server is more than just a database platform; it's a comprehensive ecosystem that supports a wide range of data-centric applications. This introduction has provided an overview of SQL Server's purpose, architecture, and applications. In the chapters that follow, we'll dive deep into specific aspects of SQL Server, with hands-on exercises and examples that demystify each concept and help you build the expertise to use SQL Server effectively.

This introductory chapter sets the stage, giving readers a foundational understanding of SQL Server and its role in today's data-driven world. With this background, they'll be well-prepared to move into installation, configuration, and eventually more advanced topics in SQL Server mastery.

CHAPTER 2: INSTALLATION AND CONFIGURATION

Overview

Installing and configuring SQL Server is the critical first step to getting started with this powerful database platform. A successful installation involves selecting the right edition, configuring essential settings, and setting up the server to ensure optimal performance and security. In this chapter, we'll guide you through the installation process step-by-step and cover key configuration options that will lay a solid foundation for using SQL Server effectively.

1. Preparing for Installation

Before diving into the installation process, it's essential to check **system requirements** to ensure compatibility and optimal performance. Here are the key prerequisites:

- **Operating System**: SQL Server is primarily designed for Windows, but certain editions also support Linux.
- **Hardware Requirements**: SQL Server requires a minimum amount of CPU, memory, and disk space. Make sure your system meets or exceeds these minimums for the edition you're installing.

- **Network Configuration**: Ensure network connectivity if SQL Server will be accessed remotely or integrated with other applications.

You'll also need to decide which **SQL Server edition** to install based on your needs (e.g., SQL Server Express for small applications, Standard for mid-sized organizations, or Enterprise for high-performance, large-scale environments).

2. Downloading SQL Server

Microsoft offers SQL Server downloads through its website. Here's how to access the installer:

1. **Visit the Microsoft SQL Server website** and select your desired version (e.g., SQL Server 2019, SQL Server 2022).
2. Choose the appropriate edition based on your use case. Free editions like SQL Server Express or Developer are available for non-production and learning purposes.

After downloading the installation media, you'll be ready to launch the SQL Server setup process.

3. Running the SQL Server Installer

Upon launching the installer, you'll be presented with several setup options. Follow these steps to ensure a smooth installation:

1. **Choose Installation Type**: Select **New SQL Server stand-alone installation** to set up a fresh instance. Alternatively, you can choose to **add features** to an existing instance.

2. **Product Key and License Terms**: Enter the product key for your edition if prompted (Developer and Express editions don't require a product key), and accept the license terms.

3. **Global Rules Check**: The installer will check your system for compatibility. Address any warnings or errors (e.g., updates, hardware requirements) to prevent installation issues.

4. **Feature Selection**: SQL Server offers a variety of features, including:

   o **Database Engine Services**: Core component for managing relational databases.

   o **SQL Server Replication**: Enables data replication across servers.

   o **Full-Text and Semantic Extractions for Search**: Enhances search capabilities within text data.

   o **Analysis Services**: Adds support for multidimensional and tabular data models.

   o **Integration Services (SSIS)**: For data integration and ETL tasks.

   o **Reporting Services (SSRS)**: Provides reporting capabilities.

Select only the necessary features for your project, as each adds to system resource requirements.

5. **Instance Configuration**: SQL Server supports multiple instances on the same machine. Choose between:
   o **Default Instance**: Identified by the server name only, typically used when only one instance is installed.
   o **Named Instance**: Allows for multiple instances with different names, each with separate settings and databases.

6. **Server Configuration**: Set up service accounts and startup types for each SQL Server component:
   o **Service Accounts**: Assign a Windows user account for each SQL Server service. Using separate accounts can enhance security.
   o **Collation Settings**: Defines how data is sorted and compared. The default collation is generally sufficient, but customizations may be necessary for specific language or locale requirements.

7. **Database Engine Configuration**:
   o **Authentication Mode**: Choose between **Windows Authentication** (for Windows-integrated security) or **Mixed Mode** (which includes SQL Server Authentication). Mixed Mode is recommended for

flexibility but requires setting a strong password for the SQL Server system administrator (SA) account.

- ○ **SQL Server Administrators**: Specify accounts with administrative privileges. It's best practice to limit this to essential users only.

8. **Data Directories and File Locations**: Configure where SQL Server stores data, log files, backups, and other essential files. Choosing high-performance storage (e.g., SSD) for critical files can improve performance.

9. **TempDB Configuration**: TempDB is a temporary workspace for SQL Server. Configure the number of TempDB files (typically one per CPU core) and allocate sufficient initial size and autogrowth settings to handle peak workload without frequent resizing.

4. Verifying and Completing the Installation

After configuring settings, SQL Server setup will perform a **summary check** and initiate the installation. Once complete, review the **installation log** for any errors or warnings, and restart the system if necessary.

5. Installing SQL Server Management Studio (SSMS)

SQL Server Management Studio (SSMS) is a critical tool for managing SQL Server instances and performing administrative tasks. To install SSMS:

1. **Download SSMS** from the Microsoft SQL Server website as a separate download.
2. Run the installer and follow the prompts to complete installation.

SSMS provides a graphical user interface to interact with SQL Server, making it easier to run queries, manage databases, and configure server settings.

6. Post-Installation Configuration

After installation, additional configurations can improve SQL Server's performance, security, and usability. These include:

- **Setting Up Network Connectivity**: Configure **TCP/IP settings** and open firewall ports if SQL Server needs to be accessible over a network.
- **Configuring SQL Server Memory**: Limit the maximum memory usage to prevent SQL Server from consuming all available system memory, which could impact other applications.
- **Setting Up Database Mail**: Enable email notifications for alerts and status updates on server performance or errors.
- **Enabling SQL Server Agent**: Start the SQL Server Agent for scheduling and automating tasks, such as backups and maintenance.

7. Testing the Installation

To confirm the SQL Server installation, connect to the server using SSMS and execute a simple test query:

1. **Launch SSMS** and connect to your SQL Server instance.
2. In a new query window, run a test query to verify that the server responds correctly:

sql

Copy code

SELECT @@VERSION;

This query returns the SQL Server version, confirming that the server is operational.

8. Common Installation Issues and Troubleshooting

During installation, some common issues may arise. Here's how to troubleshoot them:

- **Insufficient Permissions**: Ensure you have administrator rights on the system and for SQL Server services.
- **Network Configuration Errors**: Verify firewall settings and TCP/IP configurations if you encounter connectivity issues.
- **Insufficient Disk Space**: Confirm that adequate storage is available, especially for larger editions like Enterprise.

If installation fails, refer to the **SQL Server installation log** for detailed error information.

A well-planned installation and configuration of SQL Server sets the stage for efficient database management and smooth performance. This chapter has guided you through each step, from preparing your system to verifying the installation. With SQL Server up and running, you're ready to dive into creating and managing databases, writing queries, and configuring advanced features that will be covered in the following chapters.

CHAPTER 3: SQL SERVER MANAGEMENT STUDIO (SSMS) ESSENTIALS

Overview

SQL Server Management Studio (SSMS) is a powerful tool that provides a graphical interface for managing SQL Server databases, writing and executing queries, and performing administrative tasks. For database professionals, SSMS is essential as it simplifies working with SQL Server through an organized environment with user-friendly navigation and comprehensive management options. This chapter will walk you through the core features of SSMS, helping you understand how to leverage it to manage databases, streamline workflows, and maximize productivity.

1. Getting Started with SSMS

Once you've installed SSMS, you'll be greeted by the **Connect to Server** window each time you launch it. This window allows you to connect to your SQL Server instance:

- **Server Type**: Typically, this is set to "Database Engine" for SQL Server.
- **Server Name**: Enter the name of your SQL Server instance. If SSMS is installed on the same computer as SQL Server, "localhost" or "." can be used.

- **Authentication Mode**: Choose between **Windows Authentication** (uses your Windows credentials) and **SQL Server Authentication** (requires a SQL Server username and password).

After connecting to the server, SSMS will load the **Object Explorer** pane, which displays your SQL Server instance and its components, such as databases, security settings, and server objects.

2. SSMS Interface Overview

SSMS is organized into several main areas:

- **Object Explorer**: The central navigation pane that allows you to browse databases, tables, views, stored procedures, and other objects within your SQL Server instance.
- **Query Editor**: A text editor where you can write and execute SQL queries. It provides syntax highlighting, IntelliSense, and debugging tools to enhance productivity.
- **Properties Window**: Displays properties for selected objects, such as a table or database, allowing you to quickly view and edit settings.
- **Results Pane**: Shows the results of executed queries, including data returned from SELECT queries, messages, and error information.

Familiarizing yourself with each of these areas will help you navigate and use SSMS efficiently.

3. Creating and Managing Databases

SSMS makes it easy to create and manage databases without requiring complex SQL commands. Here's how to create a database in SSMS:

1. **In Object Explorer**, right-click on the **Databases** folder and select **New Database**.
2. In the **New Database** dialog, specify a name for your database.
3. Customize settings such as **initial size** and **autogrowth** settings for data and log files if needed.
4. Click **OK** to create the database.

Once' created, your database will appear in Object Explorer under the **Databases** folder. From here, you can expand the database to view and manage tables, views, stored procedures, and other database objects.

4. Working with Tables

Tables are fundamental to database design, as they store data in rows and columns. SSMS provides a straightforward interface for creating and modifying tables:

1. **Creating a Table**:
   o Right-click on the **Tables** folder within your database and select **New Table**.

o In the **Table Designer** window, define columns by specifying the **column name**, **data type**, and other constraints (e.g., **Primary Key, Allow Nulls**).

o Save the table by providing a name when prompted.

2. **Modifying a Table**:

o Right-click on the table and select **Design** to open the Table Designer.

o You can add, remove, or modify columns and constraints from here.

3. **Viewing and Editing Data**:

o Right-click on the table and choose **Select Top 1000 Rows** to view data.

o To add or modify data directly, select **Edit Top 200 Rows**.

The Table Designer in SSMS allows for efficient table creation and modification without the need to write SQL commands, although SQL scripts can still be used for advanced customization.

5. Writing and Executing Queries in Query Editor

The Query Editor in SSMS is where you can write, edit, and execute SQL queries. Key features of the Query Editor include:

• **Syntax Highlighting**: Automatically highlights keywords, making queries easier to read.

- **IntelliSense**: Provides suggestions and autocompletes code as you type, which speeds up query writing and reduces errors.
- **Query Execution**: Execute queries by pressing **F5** or clicking the **Execute** button in the toolbar.

Basic Example:

sql
Copy code
SELECT * FROM dbo.YourTable;

Executing Queries:

- Run individual queries by highlighting the SQL code you want to execute and clicking **Execute**.
- The **Results Pane** will display data for SELECT queries or indicate the success of other statements (e.g., INSERT, UPDATE).

The Query Editor is versatile, allowing you to work with complex queries and providing valuable tools like debugging and execution plans (covered in later chapters).

6. Using Templates and Snippets

SSMS includes a library of **templates** for commonly used SQL Server scripts. Templates can be a time-saver and help ensure best practices. To access templates:

1. Open the **Template Explorer** from the **View** menu.

2. Browse templates for creating tables, stored procedures, views, and other objects.

3. Double-click a template to open it in the Query Editor.

Templates are customizable, so you can adjust them to fit your specific needs and save them for future use.

7. Managing Security and Permissions

SQL Server includes robust security features that allow you to control access to databases and specific objects within them. Common security tasks in SSMS include:

- **Creating Logins**: Logins grant users access to the SQL Server instance. Right-click **Security** > **Logins** and select **New Login** to add a new user.

- **Database Users**: Assign logins to individual databases as users. In your database, go to **Security** > **Users**, right-click, and choose **New User**.

- **Permissions**: Set specific permissions (e.g., SELECT, INSERT, UPDATE) for users or roles. Right-click on a database object, select **Properties**, and configure permissions under the **Permissions** tab.

Managing security within SSMS allows you to ensure data protection and maintain compliance with access control policies.

8. Automating Tasks with SQL Server Agent

SQL Server Agent is a job scheduler in SQL Server, allowing you to automate repetitive tasks such as backups, indexing, and other maintenance operations. To set up a job:

1. **Expand SQL Server Agent** in Object Explorer.
2. Right-click **Jobs** and select **New Job**.
3. In the **New Job** dialog, specify the job name and description.
4. Add **Steps** to the job, defining specific actions (e.g., T-SQL statements) for each step.
5. Schedule the job under the **Schedules** tab, setting the frequency and timing for execution.

SQL Server Agent is a powerful tool for keeping your SQL Server environment running smoothly without manual intervention.

9. Monitoring and Troubleshooting in SSMS

SSMS provides several tools for monitoring SQL Server's health and troubleshooting issues:

- **Activity Monitor**: Provides an overview of server performance, including CPU usage, active sessions, and recent expensive queries.
- **Error Logs**: SQL Server logs errors and warnings. Access these under **Management > SQL Server Logs**.

- **Extended Events**: For more granular monitoring, use **Extended Events** to create custom event tracking. This can be configured under **Management > Extended Events**.

These tools help you monitor server health and diagnose performance issues, ensuring SQL Server runs at its best.

10. Customizing SSMS

SSMS offers a variety of customization options, allowing you to tailor the environment to your workflow:

- **Changing Fonts and Colors**: Go to **Tools > Options** to modify colors, fonts, and other display options in the Query Editor.
- **Keyboard Shortcuts**: Customize shortcuts under **Tools > Options > Keyboard** to speed up common tasks.
- **Saving Layouts**: SSMS lets you save customized layouts for Object Explorer, Properties, and other windows, so you can switch between configurations based on your workflow.

Customization in SSMS helps streamline your work, making it more efficient and comfortable.

SQL Server Management Studio is an essential tool for any SQL Server user. This chapter introduced you to SSMS, showing you how to navigate the interface, create and manage databases, write and execute queries, configure security, and monitor server health.

With a strong grasp of SSMS essentials, you're ready to dive deeper into database management and begin developing complex queries and database structures with confidence in SQL Server.

CHAPTER 4: UNDERSTANDING SQL SERVER DATABASES

Overview

A SQL Server database is more than just a collection of tables; it's a structured storage system that organizes data in a way that ensures both consistency and efficiency. To use SQL Server effectively, it's essential to understand how databases are structured, the relationships between database objects, and the core concepts that make SQL Server databases reliable and scalable. This chapter covers the anatomy of a SQL Server database, exploring components such as tables, schemas, relationships, keys, and indexes, all while providing practical examples to illustrate these concepts.

1. The Database Structure

A database in SQL Server is organized into a hierarchy of objects, with **databases** at the top level. Each database contains a series of objects that serve specific roles in data storage and retrieval. The fundamental objects within a SQL Server database are:

- **Tables**: Store data in rows and columns, functioning as the core of any relational database.
- **Schemas**: Logical containers that organize and group tables, views, and other objects.

- **Views**: Virtual tables created by querying one or more tables; they provide an abstracted layer of data.
- **Stored Procedures**: Predefined SQL code that performs specific tasks, often used to automate processes.
- **Functions**: Code that returns a value, often used for calculations or transformations on data.

Understanding the function of each object is key to designing efficient databases and writing effective queries.

2. Database Files and Filegroups

SQL Server databases are stored in physical files on disk, divided into three main types:

- **Primary Data File (.mdf)**: Contains the primary database structure and data.
- **Secondary Data File (.ndf)**: Optional files that can be used to spread data across multiple disks.
- **Transaction Log File (.ldf)**: Records all transactions, which ensures data recovery and consistency.

Databases can also use **filegroups** to organize data files. Filegroups improve performance by spreading data across multiple disks, which is useful for high-volume databases.

Example: When creating a database, you can specify additional filegroups to store specific tables or indexes, allowing SQL Server to distribute workload efficiently.

3. Schemas: Organizing Database Objects

A **schema** is a logical container within a database that groups related tables, views, and other objects. By default, SQL Server uses the dbo schema, but creating custom schemas can help with organization, security, and maintenance.

Example: In a large organization, you might create separate schemas for sales, inventory, and hr departments, grouping related tables and views under each schema. This structure can help simplify access control, as permissions can be managed at the schema level.

Creating a Schema:

```sql
Copy code
CREATE SCHEMA Sales;
```

Creating a Table in a Schema:

```sql
Copy code
CREATE TABLE Sales.Orders (
    OrderID INT PRIMARY KEY,
    CustomerID INT,
```

OrderDate DATE

);

4. Tables and Data Types

Tables are the core objects in any relational database, where data is stored in rows and columns. Designing tables requires specifying columns with the appropriate **data types** to ensure data integrity. SQL Server supports various data types, grouped into categories such as:

- **Numeric**: INT, DECIMAL, FLOAT
- **String**: VARCHAR, NVARCHAR, CHAR
- **Date and Time**: DATE, TIME, DATETIME
- **Binary**: BINARY, VARBINARY
- **Unique Identifier**: UNIQUEIDENTIFIER

Example:

sql

Copy code

```
CREATE TABLE Customers (
    CustomerID INT PRIMARY KEY,
    FirstName NVARCHAR(50),
    LastName NVARCHAR(50),
    Email NVARCHAR(100) UNIQUE,
    DateOfBirth DATE
);
```

Choosing the right data types for each column is critical for database performance, as larger data types consume more storage and affect query speed.

5. Primary Keys and Foreign Keys

Primary keys and **foreign keys** are essential for establishing relationships between tables, enforcing referential integrity within a database.

- **Primary Key**: Uniquely identifies each record in a table. Each table should have one primary key, typically a single column, like CustomerID, or a combination of columns.
- **Foreign Key**: A column in one table that links to a primary key in another table, establishing a relationship.

Example: A CustomerID column in an Orders table can be a foreign key referencing the CustomerID primary key in the Customers table. This setup ensures that every order is associated with a valid customer.

Creating a Foreign Key:

sql
Copy code

```
CREATE TABLE Orders (
    OrderID INT PRIMARY KEY,
```

CustomerID INT FOREIGN KEY REFERENCES
Customers(CustomerID),
OrderDate DATE
);

6. Relationships and Normalization

Relational databases are based on the concept of **relationships** between tables. There are three types of relationships:

- **One-to-One**: Each record in one table relates to a single record in another.
- **One-to-Many**: A record in one table relates to multiple records in another (e.g., a customer with multiple orders).
- **Many-to-Many**: Multiple records in one table relate to multiple records in another. These relationships often require a junction table.

Normalization is the process of structuring tables to minimize data redundancy. By breaking down data into multiple related tables, normalization ensures efficient storage and reduces inconsistencies.

7. Indexes for Performance Optimization

Indexes in SQL Server improve query performance by organizing data in a way that makes retrieval faster. Common types of indexes include:

- **Clustered Index**: Physically sorts and stores data based on the indexed column(s). Each table can have only one clustered index.
- **Non-Clustered Index**: Creates a separate structure that points to the data, allowing multiple indexes per table.

Example: To improve performance when searching for customers by LastName, you could create a non-clustered index:

sql
Copy code

```
CREATE NONCLUSTERED INDEX idx_LastName
ON Customers (LastName);
```

Indexes are powerful but should be used thoughtfully, as they increase storage requirements and can slow down insert and update operations.

8. Views: Abstracting and Simplifying Data Access

A **view** is a virtual table that provides a custom, simplified perspective of data by running a query against one or more tables. Views can be used to hide complex joins, filter sensitive information, or create pre-aggregated data for faster retrieval.

Example:

sql
Copy code

```
CREATE VIEW SalesSummary AS
```

```
SELECT CustomerID, COUNT(OrderID) AS TotalOrders,
SUM(OrderAmount) AS TotalSales
FROM Orders
GROUP BY CustomerID;
```

Using views can make data easier to work with, especially for end-users who need limited access to specific data.

9. Stored Procedures and Functions

Stored Procedures are reusable SQL scripts saved in the database, which can perform complex tasks or automate repetitive operations. **Functions** are similar but typically return a single value and are used for calculations or transformations.

Example of a Stored Procedure:

```sql
Copy code
CREATE PROCEDURE GetCustomerOrders
    @CustomerID INT
AS
BEGIN
    SELECT * FROM Orders WHERE CustomerID = @CustomerID;
END;
```

Stored procedures help in code reusability, security, and efficiency, especially for tasks like data manipulation and batch processing.

10. Constraints for Data Integrity

SQL Server offers constraints to enforce rules at the database level, ensuring that data remains accurate and consistent:

- **PRIMARY KEY**: Ensures unique values in a column.
- **FOREIGN KEY**: Enforces referential integrity.
- **UNIQUE**: Ensures all values in a column are distinct.
- **CHECK**: Enforces specific conditions for column values.
- **DEFAULT**: Provides a default value if no other value is specified.

Example of a CHECK Constraint:

sql

Copy code

```
CREATE TABLE Employees (
    EmployeeID INT PRIMARY KEY,
    Age INT CHECK (Age >= 18),
    Salary DECIMAL(10, 2) CHECK (Salary > 0)
);
```

Using constraints maintains data accuracy and reduces the need for manual data validation in applications.

Understanding the structure and components of a SQL Server database is crucial to working effectively with relational data. In this chapter, we explored the anatomy of a SQL Server database, including tables, schemas, relationships, indexes, views, and stored procedures, with a focus on best practices for data integrity and efficiency. With this knowledge, you are well-prepared to start creating databases, designing schemas, and implementing relationships that will form the foundation of your data-driven applications. In the next chapter, we'll dive into database design and modeling, guiding you on how to build an optimized database from the ground up.

CHAPTER 5: DATA TYPES AND TABLE DESIGN

Overview

In SQL Server, designing tables with the right structure and choosing appropriate data types are foundational for a well-functioning database. The data types you choose affect storage efficiency, data integrity, and query performance, while a carefully planned table design helps you organize information in a way that's both logical and scalable. In this chapter, we'll explore SQL Server's data types in detail and discuss best practices for designing tables that support efficient, reliable, and easy-to-maintain databases.

1. Importance of Choosing the Right Data Types

The choice of data types has a significant impact on the database's performance and storage requirements. Using a data type that's too large (e.g., using INT instead of SMALLINT when storing small numbers) wastes storage, while using an overly restrictive data type (e.g., CHAR(10) for names) can lead to data truncation or compromise flexibility. Selecting the correct data type ensures that your tables store data efficiently while maintaining accuracy.

When choosing data types, consider:

- The **range of values** that needs to be stored.
- The **precision** needed for numeric data.

- **Storage efficiency** for larger datasets.
- **Compatibility** with other data sources.

2. Common SQL Server Data Types

SQL Server offers a wide range of data types categorized into several types: numeric, string, date/time, and binary. Let's explore the most commonly used types in each category.

Numeric Data Types

- **INT**: Stores whole numbers between -2,147,483,648 and 2,147,483,647. Often used for identifiers or counters.
- **SMALLINT**: Uses half the storage of INT, for values between -32,768 and 32,767.
- **BIGINT**: For very large integers, with a range of -9,223,372,036,854,775,808 to 9,223,372,036,854,775,807.
- **DECIMAL(p, s) / NUMERIC(p, s)**: For precise fixed-point numbers, where p is the precision (total number of digits) and s is the scale (digits after the decimal).
- **FLOAT / REAL**: For approximate floating-point numbers, useful for scientific or statistical data.

String Data Types

- **CHAR(n)**: Fixed-length string; always uses the defined number of characters. Ideal for fields with a consistent length, like state codes.

- **VARCHAR(n)**: Variable-length string, where n defines the maximum length. Ideal for text fields like names or addresses.
- **TEXT**: Stores large amounts of text, but it's generally recommended to use VARCHAR(MAX) for more flexibility.

Date and Time Data Types

- **DATE**: Stores only the date, without time.
- **TIME**: Stores only the time, without date.
- **DATETIME**: Stores both date and time, accurate to the second.
- **DATETIME2**: Similar to DATETIME, but allows higher precision and a broader range.
- **SMALLDATETIME**: Stores both date and time, but with limited range and precision.
- **TIMESTAMP**: Unique binary number within the database, often used for row versioning.

Binary Data Types

- **BINARY(n)**: Fixed-length binary data, useful for data like hashes.
- **VARBINARY(n)**: Variable-length binary data, often used for images or files.

- **VARBINARY(MAX)**: Can store larger binary objects up to 2 GB.

Other Data Types

- **UNIQUEIDENTIFIER**: A 16-byte globally unique identifier (GUID), often used for unique keys.
- **BIT**: Stores 0, 1, or NULL. Efficient for Boolean data (e.g., Yes/No or True/False fields).
- **XML**: Stores XML-formatted data.
- **JSON** (only through NVARCHAR(MAX)): While not a native type, JSON can be stored as text in SQL Server, enabling JSON parsing functions.

3. Best Practices for Data Type Selection

Choosing data types with storage efficiency and performance in mind is critical:

- **Use appropriate precision** for numbers: Avoid using FLOAT or DECIMAL with excessive precision unless necessary, as they require more storage.
- **Limit VARCHAR size**: Specify the maximum expected length for VARCHAR columns to optimize storage. For text that could exceed 8000 characters, use VARCHAR(MAX).
- **Use appropriate date/time types**: If you only need the date or time, choose DATE or TIME rather than DATETIME.

- **Avoid using large types unnecessarily**: For instance, use INT instead of BIGINT if values fall within the INT range.

4. Designing Tables: Structure and Layout

When designing a table, aim to create a structure that's both efficient and logical. This process involves defining columns, setting constraints, and normalizing data.

Creating a Table: The basic syntax for creating a table involves defining columns with data types and any optional constraints.

sql
Copy code
```
CREATE TABLE Employees (
    EmployeeID INT PRIMARY KEY,
    FirstName NVARCHAR(50),
    LastName NVARCHAR(50),
    DateOfBirth DATE,
    Salary DECIMAL(10, 2),
    IsActive BIT
);
```
In this example:

- EmployeeID serves as a primary key.
- FirstName and LastName use NVARCHAR to support multi-language characters.
- DateOfBirth uses DATE to store only the date.

- Salary uses DECIMAL(10, 2) for precise numeric storage.
- IsActive uses BIT for Boolean data.

Setting Default Values: You can assign a default value to a column, which SQL Server uses if no other value is provided.

sql

Copy code

```
CREATE TABLE Orders (
    OrderID INT PRIMARY KEY,
    OrderDate DATETIME DEFAULT GETDATE(),
    Status VARCHAR(20) DEFAULT 'Pending'
);
```

5. Constraints for Data Integrity

Constraints enforce rules on data in a table, ensuring data integrity and preventing invalid data entry.

- **PRIMARY KEY**: Uniquely identifies each record in a table. A primary key automatically creates a unique index.
- **FOREIGN KEY**: Establishes a relationship between two tables, linking records in one table to those in another.
- **UNIQUE**: Ensures all values in a column are unique.
- **CHECK**: Specifies conditions that must be met for a value to be valid.
- **DEFAULT**: Provides a default value when no value is specified for a column.

- **NOT NULL**: Ensures that a column always has a value.

Example with Constraints:

sql

Copy code

```
CREATE TABLE Products (
    ProductID INT PRIMARY KEY,
    ProductName NVARCHAR(100) NOT NULL,
    Price DECIMAL(10, 2) CHECK (Price > 0),
    StockQuantity INT DEFAULT 0,
    CategoryID INT FOREIGN KEY REFERENCES
Categories(CategoryID)
);
```

6. Normalization: Designing Efficient Table Structures

Normalization is the process of structuring tables to minimize redundancy and dependency. The main goal is to split data into related tables to reduce duplicate information and make updates more efficient.

Normalization Levels:

1. **First Normal Form (1NF)**: Ensure each column holds atomic values (one value per column).

2. **Second Normal Form (2NF)**: Achieve 1NF and ensure no partial dependencies, meaning non-key columns should depend on the entire primary key.

3. **Third Normal Form (3NF)**: Achieve 2NF and remove transitive dependencies, ensuring non-key columns don't depend on other non-key columns.

Example of Normalization: Instead of storing the CustomerName in each Order record, create a Customers table and link Orders to it via CustomerID.

Customers Table:

sql

Copy code

```
CREATE TABLE Customers (
    CustomerID INT PRIMARY KEY,
    CustomerName NVARCHAR(100)
);
```

Orders Table:

sql

Copy code

```
CREATE TABLE Orders (
    OrderID INT PRIMARY KEY,
    CustomerID INT FOREIGN KEY REFERENCES Customers(CustomerID),
```

OrderDate DATE

);

7. Denormalization for Performance

While normalization is essential for efficient data management, **denormalization** can improve performance in read-heavy applications. Denormalization involves duplicating data across tables to reduce the number of joins required for queries.

For instance, storing the CustomerName in the Orders table can speed up queries that frequently access customer and order data together.

8. Indexing Strategies for Optimized Table Design

Indexes improve data retrieval speed, especially for large tables. However, too many indexes can slow down data modification operations (inserts, updates, and deletes). Strategic indexing is essential for balancing performance.

- **Clustered Index**: Determines the physical order of data. Each table can have only one clustered index, typically on the primary key.
- **Non-Clustered Index**: A separate structure that points to data rows. Useful for frequently searched columns.

Creating an Index:

sql

Copy code

```
CREATE NONCLUSTERED INDEX idx_LastName
ON Employees (LastName);
```

9. Partitioning for Large Tables

For extremely large tables, **partitioning** can improve query performance by dividing data into manageable segments, typically based on a column like Date or Region. SQL Server's partitioning feature allows efficient access to data subsets without the overhead of full table scans.

Example of a Partitioned Table: Partition an orders table by year, creating separate storage for each year's orders, which can be helpful for performance on queries that frequently filter by date.

Choosing the right data types and designing tables thoughtfully are essential steps in building a well-optimized SQL Server database. This chapter covered how to select data types that balance storage efficiency with performance, implement constraints to enforce data integrity, and design normalized tables that reduce redundancy. With a strong foundation in table design and data types, you're ready to start creating tables that support efficient and reliable data management, setting the stage for complex database operations and advanced querying. In the next chapter, we'll dive into writing basic SQL queries to retrieve and manipulate data from these tables.

CHAPTER 6: WRITING BASIC SQL QUERIES

Overview

Writing SQL queries is fundamental to working with SQL Server, as it allows you to retrieve, update, and manipulate data in your database. This chapter will cover the basics of SQL queries, focusing on key commands such as SELECT, INSERT, UPDATE, and DELETE. We'll also explore how to filter, sort, and join data from multiple tables, providing examples along the way to help you understand how each command works in real-world scenarios.

1. The Structure of a SQL Query

A SQL query typically follows a specific structure, especially for data retrieval commands:

sql

SELECT column1, column2, ...

FROM table_name

WHERE condition

ORDER BY column;

Let's break down each part:

- **SELECT**: Specifies the columns to retrieve.
- **FROM**: Indicates the table from which to retrieve data.
- **WHERE**: Filters data based on conditions.

- **ORDER BY**: Sorts the results by one or more columns.

This structure provides the foundation for querying data, and each clause can be expanded or modified to perform more complex operations.

2. Basic Data Retrieval with SELECT

The SELECT statement is used to retrieve data from a table. Here's an example that retrieves all columns from a table named Employees:

sql

SELECT * FROM Employees;

In this query, the * symbol means "all columns." To retrieve specific columns, simply list them after SELECT:

sql

SELECT FirstName, LastName, Department

FROM Employees;

Example Use Case: Suppose you want to see just the first and last names of all employees without unnecessary details. Using specific column names reduces data transfer and makes the output more readable.

3. Filtering Data with WHERE

The WHERE clause filters records based on a condition, allowing you to retrieve only the data you need. Here's an example that selects employees who work in the "Sales" department:

```sql
SELECT FirstName, LastName
FROM Employees
WHERE Department = 'Sales';
```

Comparison Operators:

- =: Equal to
- <> or !=: Not equal to
- <, >, <=, >=: Less than, greater than, etc.

Example with Multiple Conditions:

```sql
SELECT FirstName, LastName, Salary
FROM Employees
WHERE Department = 'Sales' AND Salary > 50000;
```

The AND operator combines conditions, while the OR operator allows multiple alternatives. Using conditions efficiently narrows down large datasets, returning only relevant results.

4. Sorting Results with ORDER BY

The ORDER BY clause sorts the results in ascending (default) or descending order. Here's an example that retrieves employee names and sorts them by last name:

```sql
SELECT FirstName, LastName
```

FROM Employees

ORDER BY LastName;

To sort in descending order, use the DESC keyword:

sql

SELECT FirstName, LastName

FROM Employees

ORDER BY LastName DESC;

Example Use Case: When analyzing sales data, you might sort by the SalesAmount column in descending order to see top-performing sales first.

5. Using Aggregate Functions for Summary Data

SQL provides several aggregate functions to perform calculations on data:

- **COUNT()**: Counts the number of rows.
- **SUM()**: Calculates the total for a column.
- **AVG()**: Calculates the average.
- **MIN()** and **MAX()**: Retrieve the minimum or maximum value.

Example: Counting the number of employees in each department.

sql

SELECT Department, COUNT(*) AS EmployeeCount

FROM Employees

GROUP BY Department;

In this query, GROUP BY groups records by the department, and COUNT(*) counts the number of employees in each group.

6. *Grouping Data with GROUP BY*

The GROUP BY clause groups records that share the same values in specified columns. It's often used with aggregate functions to summarize data.

Example: Calculate the average salary in each department.

sql
SELECT Department, AVG(Salary) AS AvgSalary
FROM Employees
GROUP BY Department;

The GROUP BY clause ensures each department has a single row with the average salary, helping with quick summaries.

7. *Filtering Groups with HAVING*

The HAVING clause filters groups created by GROUP BY. Unlike WHERE, which filters rows before aggregation, HAVING filters after aggregation.

Example: Find departments with more than 10 employees.

sql
SELECT Department, COUNT(*) AS EmployeeCount
FROM Employees

GROUP BY Department

HAVING COUNT(*) > 10;

This query first groups employees by department and then uses HAVING to show only departments with more than 10 employees.

8. Retrieving Data from Multiple Tables with JOIN

SQL joins combine rows from two or more tables based on a related column. Common types of joins include:

- **INNER JOIN**: Returns only matching rows from both tables.
- **LEFT JOIN**: Returns all rows from the left table and matching rows from the right.
- **RIGHT JOIN**: Returns all rows from the right table and matching rows from the left.
- **FULL JOIN**: Returns all rows from both tables, with unmatched rows showing as NULL.

Example of INNER JOIN: Retrieve employee names along with their department names, stored in a separate Departments table.

sql

SELECT Employees.FirstName, Employees.LastName, Departments.DepartmentName

FROM Employees

INNER JOIN Departments ON Employees.DepartmentID = Departments.DepartmentID;

In this query, INNER JOIN combines Employees and Departments based on matching DepartmentID values.

9. Inserting Data with INSERT INTO

The INSERT INTO statement adds new rows to a table. You can insert data into all columns or only specific columns.

Inserting into All Columns:

sql

Copy code

```
INSERT INTO Employees (EmployeeID, FirstName, LastName, Department, Salary)
VALUES (101, 'John', 'Doe', 'Sales', 60000);
```

Inserting into Specific Columns:

sql

```
INSERT INTO Employees (FirstName, LastName, Department)
VALUES ('Jane', 'Smith', 'Marketing');
```

In this example, only the specified columns receive values, while others may use default values or allow NULL.

10. Updating Data with UPDATE

The UPDATE statement modifies existing data in a table. To avoid accidental updates, always use a WHERE clause to specify the records to update.

Example: Increase the salary for employees in the Sales department.

sql

```
UPDATE Employees
SET Salary = Salary * 1.10
WHERE Department = 'Sales';
```

This query multiplies the salary of all Sales employees by 1.10, effectively giving them a 10% raise.

11. Deleting Data with DELETE

The DELETE statement removes rows from a table. Like UPDATE, using a WHERE clause is crucial to target specific rows.

Example: Delete employees who have left the company.

sql

Copy code

```
DELETE FROM Employees
WHERE IsActive = 0;
```

This query deletes records where the IsActive column is 0, indicating inactive employees. Without a WHERE clause, DELETE will remove all rows in the table.

12. Using Aliases for Clarity

Aliases provide temporary names for columns or tables, making queries clearer and easier to read.

Example with Column Alias:

sql

SELECT FirstName AS FName, LastName AS LName

FROM Employees;

Example with Table Alias:

sql

SELECT e.FirstName, e.LastName, d.DepartmentName

FROM Employees AS e

INNER JOIN Departments AS d ON e.DepartmentID = d.DepartmentID;

Using AS allows you to create meaningful abbreviations that simplify complex queries.

13. Practical Example: Writing a Full Query

Let's put these concepts together in a more complex example. Suppose we want to retrieve the top 5 employees with the highest salaries in the Sales department, showing their names, salaries, and department names.

sql

Copy code

SELECT e.FirstName, e.LastName, e.Salary, d.DepartmentName

FROM Employees AS e

INNER JOIN Departments AS d ON e.DepartmentID = d.DepartmentID

WHERE d.DepartmentName = 'Sales'

ORDER BY e.Salary DESC

OFFSET 0 ROWS FETCH NEXT 5 ROWS ONLY;

In this query:

- We join Employees and Departments to get department names.
- We filter results to only include employees in Sales.
- We sort by salary in descending order and use OFFSET and FETCH to limit the results to the top 5 highest salaries.

This chapter introduced you to essential SQL commands for querying, filtering, and manipulating data in SQL Server. Understanding these basic queries provides a strong foundation for more advanced operations, such as complex joins, subqueries, and data transformations. With these skills, you're ready to retrieve and manage data effectively, enabling you to make data-driven decisions and interact confidently with SQL Server databases. Next, we'll dive into advanced SQL query techniques, exploring ways to optimize and extend your queries for more powerful data analysis.

CHAPTER 7: ADVANCED SQL QUERY TECHNIQUES

Overview

Once you've mastered basic SQL queries, you can start exploring advanced query techniques to handle complex data manipulation, improve performance, and execute intricate analyses. Advanced SQL techniques include subqueries, window functions, common table expressions (CTEs), and various optimization strategies. These tools enable you to perform deeper analyses, create more efficient queries, and unlock the full power of SQL Server.

1. Subqueries for Nested Queries

A **subquery** is a query within another query. Subqueries are often used to filter results, calculate values, or perform lookups in a way that simplifies the main query.

Types of Subqueries:

- **Scalar Subquery**: Returns a single value, often used in SELECT or WHERE clauses.
- **Table Subquery**: Returns multiple rows and columns, typically used in FROM clauses.
- **Correlated Subquery**: Depends on values from the outer query, recalculating for each row.

Example: Find employees whose salary is above the company's average salary.

sql

Copy code

```
SELECT FirstName, LastName, Salary
FROM Employees
WHERE Salary > (SELECT AVG(Salary) FROM Employees);
```

In this example, the subquery (SELECT AVG(Salary) FROM Employees) calculates the average salary, and the outer query retrieves employees whose salaries exceed this average.

2. Common Table Expressions (CTEs)

Common Table Expressions (CTEs) provide a way to define temporary result sets that can be referenced within a single SELECT, INSERT, UPDATE, or DELETE statement. CTEs are particularly useful for breaking down complex queries.

Syntax:

sql

```
WITH CTE_Name AS (
   SELECT column1, column2
   FROM table_name
   WHERE condition
)
SELECT * FROM CTE_Name;
```

Example: Use a CTE to find the top 3 highest-paid employees in each department.

```sql
sql
WITH RankedSalaries AS (
    SELECT FirstName, LastName, DepartmentID, Salary,
        RANK() OVER(PARTITION BY DepartmentID ORDER BY Salary DESC) AS SalaryRank
    FROM Employees
)
SELECT FirstName, LastName, DepartmentID, Salary
FROM RankedSalaries
WHERE SalaryRank <= 3;
```

In this example, the CTE RankedSalaries assigns a rank to each employee within their department based on salary. The outer query retrieves the top 3 employees from each department by filtering on SalaryRank.

3. Window Functions for Advanced Analytics

Window functions perform calculations across a set of table rows related to the current row. Unlike aggregate functions, window functions don't collapse rows into single results, making them ideal for cumulative calculations, running totals, and rankings.

Types of Window Functions:

- **ROW_NUMBER()**: Assigns a unique sequential number to rows within a partition.
- **RANK()** and **DENSE_RANK()**: Assigns ranks to rows within a partition, with ties in ranking.
- **NTILE(n)**: Distributes rows into a specified number of groups.
- **SUM(), AVG(), MIN(), MAX()** (with OVER clause): Calculates aggregates within a window.

Example: Find the cumulative sales for each salesperson.

sql

```
SELECT SalespersonID, SaleDate, SaleAmount,
    SUM(SaleAmount) OVER(PARTITION BY SalespersonID
ORDER BY SaleDate) AS CumulativeSales
FROM Sales;
```

Here, SUM(SaleAmount) OVER(PARTITION BY SalespersonID ORDER BY SaleDate) calculates cumulative sales for each salesperson over time.

4. Using CASE Statements for Conditional Logic

The CASE statement allows you to add conditional logic to your queries, performing calculations or setting values based on conditions.

Syntax:

sql

Copy code

```
SELECT column1,
    CASE
        WHEN condition1 THEN result1
        WHEN condition2 THEN result2
        ELSE default_result
    END AS new_column
FROM table_name;
```

Example: Categorize employees by salary level.

sql

```
SELECT FirstName, LastName, Salary,
    CASE
        WHEN Salary < 50000 THEN 'Low'
        WHEN Salary BETWEEN 50000 AND 80000 THEN 'Medium'
        ELSE 'High'
    END AS SalaryLevel
FROM Employees;
```

This query adds a column SalaryLevel based on the employee's salary, making data easier to analyze.

5. PIVOT and UNPIVOT for Data Transformation

PIVOT and **UNPIVOT** are used to transform data by rotating rows into columns (PIVOT) and vice versa (UNPIVOT).

Example of PIVOT: Show total sales for each quarter by product.

sql

```
SELECT ProductID, Q1, Q2, Q3, Q4
FROM (
    SELECT ProductID, SaleAmount, DATEPART(QUARTER,
SaleDate) AS SaleQuarter
    FROM Sales
) AS SourceTable
PIVOT (
    SUM(SaleAmount)
    FOR SaleQuarter IN (Q1, Q2, Q3, Q4)
) AS PivotTable;
```

In this example, the PIVOT operator creates separate columns for each quarter, showing sales totals per product.

6. Recursive Queries with Recursive CTEs

Recursive CTEs allow you to perform recursive operations like hierarchical data retrieval, useful for scenarios like organizational charts or folder structures.

Syntax:

sql

```
WITH RecursiveCTE AS (
    SELECT column1, column2
    FROM table_name
    WHERE condition -- Base case
```

```
    UNION ALL

    SELECT column1, column2
    FROM RecursiveCTE
    JOIN table_name ON condition -- Recursive case
)
SELECT * FROM RecursiveCTE;
```

Example: Retrieve an employee hierarchy.

sql
```
WITH EmployeeHierarchy AS (
    SELECT EmployeeID, ManagerID, FirstName, LastName, 1 AS
Level
    FROM Employees
    WHERE ManagerID IS NULL -- Top-level manager

    UNION ALL

    SELECT    e.EmployeeID,    e.ManagerID,    e.FirstName,
e.LastName, eh.Level + 1
    FROM Employees e
    INNER JOIN EmployeeHierarchy eh ON e.ManagerID =
eh.EmployeeID
)
SELECT * FROM EmployeeHierarchy;
```

In this example, the recursive CTE EmployeeHierarchy builds an organizational chart, showing each employee's level relative to the top manager.

7. Optimizing Query Performance with Indexes and Execution Plans

Complex queries can slow down performance if not optimized. Here are strategies for improving query performance:

- **Indexes**: Indexes improve query speed by organizing data, but too many indexes can slow down data modification operations.
- **Execution Plans**: An execution plan shows how SQL Server executes a query, including which indexes and joins it uses. To view an execution plan in SSMS, select **Display Actual Execution Plan** before running the query. Look for:
  - **Table Scans**: Avoid if possible, as they indicate SQL Server reads the entire table. Use indexes to reduce full scans.
  - **Index Seeks**: Preferred over scans, as they retrieve specific rows efficiently.
  - **Join Types**: Make sure SQL Server uses efficient join types like **Nested Loops** or **Merge Joins** where possible.

8. Temporary Tables and Table Variables

Temporary tables and **table variables** store intermediate results for use in complex queries, ideal for breaking down large queries or storing intermediate calculations.

Creating a Temporary Table:

sql

```
CREATE TABLE #TempTable (Column1 INT, Column2 NVARCHAR(50));
INSERT INTO #TempTable (Column1, Column2) VALUES (1, 'Example');
```

Using Table Variables:

sql

Copy code

```
DECLARE @TempTable TABLE (Column1 INT, Column2 NVARCHAR(50));
INSERT INTO @TempTable (Column1, Column2) VALUES (1, 'Example');
```

Temporary tables are stored in tempdb and support indexes, while table variables are stored in memory, making them faster for small datasets.

9. Using CROSS APPLY and OUTER APPLY for Complex Joins

CROSS APPLY and **OUTER APPLY** join each row from the left table to a set of rows returned by a table-valued function on the right, useful for complex row-by-row processing.

Example: Retrieve recent orders for each customer using CROSS APPLY.

sql

```
SELECT c.CustomerID, c.CustomerName, o.OrderID, o.OrderDate
FROM Customers c
CROSS APPLY (
    SELECT TOP 1 OrderID, OrderDate
    FROM Orders o
    WHERE o.CustomerID = c.CustomerID
    ORDER BY OrderDate DESC
) AS RecentOrder;
```

In this example, CROSS APPLY retrieves the most recent order for each customer.

10. Advanced Filtering with EXISTS and NOT EXISTS

EXISTS and NOT EXISTS test for the existence of rows returned by a subquery, often providing better performance than IN or NOT IN for large datasets.

Example: Find customers who have placed orders.

sql

```
SELECT CustomerID, CustomerName
FROM Customers c
WHERE EXISTS (
    SELECT 1
```

```
  FROM Orders o
  WHERE o.CustomerID = c.CustomerID
);
```

This query returns customers with at least one order, using EXISTS to verify each customer's existence in the Orders table.

Advanced SQL techniques open up new possibilities for complex data retrieval and manipulation. This chapter covered essential tools like subqueries, CTEs, window functions, and joins, providing powerful methods for analyzing data and optimizing performance. With these advanced skills, you'll be equipped to handle complex data challenges in SQL Server, write efficient queries, and deliver high-quality results. The next chapter will explore indexes and performance optimization techniques, building on what you've learned to ensure SQL Server performs at its best.

CHAPTER 8: INDEXES AND PERFORMANCE OPTIMIZATION

Overview

Indexes are one of the most effective tools for optimizing query performance in SQL Server. By providing structured paths to data, indexes allow SQL Server to retrieve rows much faster than without them. However, improper indexing can lead to slow performance, especially for data modification operations. This chapter will cover the types of indexes available in SQL Server, strategies for choosing the right indexes, and various performance optimization techniques to ensure your queries run efficiently.

1. Understanding Indexes in SQL Server

An **index** is a data structure that improves the speed of data retrieval by creating a "roadmap" to quickly locate rows based on key values. Indexes are particularly beneficial for queries with WHERE clauses, joins, and sorting operations. SQL Server automatically creates an index on primary keys, but additional indexes can significantly improve query performance.

Types of Indexes:

- **Clustered Index**: Determines the physical order of data in a table. Each table can have only one clustered index, as it directly affects how data is stored.

- **Non-Clustered Index**: A separate structure that points to data rows. Non-clustered indexes don't affect the physical order of data, allowing each table to have multiple non-clustered indexes.

- **Unique Index**: Ensures all values in the indexed column are unique. Useful for columns that require uniqueness, such as email addresses.

- **Full-Text Index**: Supports full-text searches for large text fields, allowing for more flexible search options.

- **Filtered Index**: An optimized non-clustered index that applies to a subset of rows based on a filter condition, which is beneficial for queries with specific criteria.

2. Creating and Managing Indexes

Indexes can be created when defining a table or added later. Here's the syntax for creating common types of indexes.

Creating a Clustered Index:

sql

```
CREATE CLUSTERED INDEX idx_EmployeeID ON Employees (EmployeeID);
```

Creating a Non-Clustered Index:

sql
Copy code

CREATE NONCLUSTERED INDEX idx_LastName ON Employees (LastName);

Creating a Unique Index:

sql

CREATE UNIQUE INDEX idx_Email ON Employees (Email);

Creating a Filtered Index:

sql

CREATE NONCLUSTERED INDEX idx_ActiveEmployees ON Employees (IsActive)

WHERE IsActive = 1;

Example Use Case: Suppose most queries filter employees who are active (IsActive = 1). A filtered index on IsActive improves performance by indexing only active employees, reducing index size and scan time.

3. Indexing Strategies for Optimal Performance

Proper indexing requires a strategic approach, as too many indexes can negatively impact performance during INSERT, UPDATE, and DELETE operations.

Index Columns Used in WHERE Clauses: Prioritize indexing columns frequently used in WHERE conditions to minimize the need for full table scans.

Composite Indexes: When queries filter or sort on multiple columns, a composite index (an index on multiple columns) can improve performance.

sql
CREATE NONCLUSTERED INDEX idx_LastName_FirstName
ON Employees (LastName, FirstName);
Example: If a query frequently retrieves employees based on both LastName and FirstName, a composite index improves performance by indexing the combined key.

Avoid Over-Indexing: While indexes can improve query performance, they add overhead to data modification operations. Use only the indexes that are necessary to support common queries.

Index Selectivity: High-selectivity indexes (columns with many unique values, like EmployeeID) are more effective than low-selectivity indexes (columns with few unique values, like IsActive).

4. Using Execution Plans to Analyze Query Performance

Execution plans show how SQL Server executes queries, providing insights into optimization opportunities. In SQL Server Management Studio (SSMS), you can view the execution plan by selecting **Display Actual Execution Plan** before running a query.

Common Execution Plan Operators:

- **Index Seek**: Efficient; retrieves specific rows directly from an index. Preferable for selective queries.
- **Index Scan**: Scans the entire index, which is slower than an index seek. Scans are often necessary for low-selectivity indexes.
- **Table Scan**: Reads all rows in a table, which can be slow for large tables. Use indexes to avoid full table scans.
- **Nested Loops Join**: Efficient for small datasets or indexed joins. SQL Server processes one row at a time.
- **Hash Join**: Suitable for large datasets, as SQL Server uses hashing to match rows.

By analyzing execution plans, you can identify bottlenecks, like table scans or inefficient join types, and make adjustments to indexes or query structure.

5. Query Optimization Techniques

In addition to indexing, several query optimization techniques can improve performance:

- **Use of Appropriate Operators**: For example, use = rather than LIKE for exact matches, and avoid NOT IN for large datasets in favor of NOT EXISTS.
- **Avoid Using Functions in WHERE Clauses**: Applying functions to columns in WHERE clauses (e.g., WHERE YEAR(OrderDate) = 2023) prevents SQL Server from using

indexes efficiently. Instead, rewrite the condition to allow index usage (e.g., WHERE OrderDate >= '2023-01-01' AND OrderDate < '2024-01-01').

- **Use Joins Instead of Subqueries Where Possible**: Joins are generally more efficient than subqueries, especially for large datasets.
- **Limit Data with SELECT TOP**: Use SELECT TOP n to limit the result set when you only need a subset of rows.

Example:

sql
```
SELECT TOP 10 FirstName, LastName, Salary
FROM Employees
ORDER BY Salary DESC;
```
This query returns the top 10 highest-paid employees, improving performance by reducing the dataset size.

6. Avoiding Common Indexing Pitfalls

There are a few common mistakes to avoid when working with indexes:

- **Over-Indexing**: Too many indexes can slow down data modification operations. Focus on indexes that benefit the most frequently used queries.
- **Ignoring Maintenance**: Indexes can become fragmented over time, leading to slower query performance. Regular

index maintenance, including rebuilding or reorganizing indexes, is essential.

- **Non-Selective Indexes**: Indexes on low-selectivity columns (columns with few unique values) may provide little to no performance gain and consume unnecessary storage.

- **Not Analyzing Query Patterns**: Indexing should be based on actual query patterns, not assumptions. Regularly review and refine indexes based on common queries and execution plans.

7. Index Maintenance: Rebuilding and Reorganizing

Indexes can become fragmented as data is inserted, updated, and deleted, which can slow down read performance. SQL Server provides two options to manage index fragmentation:

- **Reorganizing**: A lightweight operation that compacts index pages without rebuilding the entire structure.

```sql
ALTER INDEX idx_LastName ON Employees REORGANIZE;
```

- **Rebuilding**: Creates a new index structure, which removes fragmentation and reclaims unused space. This operation can be resource-intensive but provides better performance improvements.

sql

ALTER INDEX idx_LastName ON Employees REBUILD;

It's good practice to reorganize or rebuild indexes periodically, especially for heavily modified tables.

8. Using Statistics to Improve Query Performance

SQL Server uses **statistics** to make informed decisions about query execution. Statistics track data distribution in indexed columns, helping SQL Server choose the best indexes and join strategies. Outdated statistics can lead to poor query performance.

Updating Statistics:

sql

UPDATE STATISTICS Employees;

You can also enable automatic statistics updates in SQL Server, but for large tables or high-volume queries, manually updating statistics may yield better results.

9. Partitioning for Large Tables

Partitioning divides large tables or indexes into smaller, more manageable segments based on a specified column, such as a date. Partitioning improves performance by allowing SQL Server to scan only relevant segments rather than the entire table.

Example of Partitioned Table: Partitioning a sales table by year can reduce scan times for queries that filter on OrderDate.

Benefits of Partitioning:

- **Improved Query Performance**: SQL Server can quickly access partitions relevant to a query.
- **Efficient Data Management**: You can archive or delete old partitions without affecting active data.
- **Faster Index Maintenance**: Indexes can be maintained on specific partitions rather than the entire table.

Partitioning is typically used for very large tables and can improve performance significantly in data warehouse scenarios.

10. Using Temporary Tables and Table Variables for Intermediate Results

Temporary tables and **table variables** are useful for breaking down complex queries, storing intermediate results, and improving readability. However, they should be used with caution, as excessive use can lead to performance issues.

Temporary Tables: Created with a # prefix, temporary tables are stored in tempdb, allowing for indexing and flexibility.

sql
```
CREATE TABLE #TempResults (Column1 INT, Column2 NVARCHAR(50));
```

Table Variables: Declared with DECLARE, table variables are stored in memory, making them faster for small datasets but limited in performance and flexibility.

sql

DECLARE @TempTable TABLE (Column1 INT, Column2 NVARCHAR(50));

Use temporary tables for large datasets that require indexing, and use table variables for smaller datasets or when indexing isn't required.

11. Monitoring and Troubleshooting Performance with Dynamic Management Views (DMVs)

Dynamic Management Views (DMVs) provide insights into SQL Server's health, performance, and resource usage. Key DMVs for monitoring indexes and queries include:

- **sys.dm_db_index_usage_stats**: Shows how frequently indexes are used, helping you identify unused or redundant indexes.
- **sys.dm_exec_query_stats**: Provides execution statistics for cached queries, helping you identify slow-running queries.
- **sys.dm_exec_query_plan**: Shows the execution plan for cached queries, allowing for detailed analysis of query performance.

Example: Identify indexes that are rarely used.

sql

Copy code

```
SELECT OBJECT_NAME(i.object_id) AS TableName, i.name AS
IndexName,
    ius.user_seeks,     ius.user_scans,     ius.user_lookups,
ius.user_updates
FROM sys.indexes AS i
JOIN sys.dm_db_index_usage_stats AS ius
ON i.index_id = ius.index_id
WHERE    ius.database_id    =    DB_ID('YourDatabase')    AND
ius.user_seeks = 0;
```

This query helps identify indexes with zero seeks, indicating they may be candidates for removal.

Indexes and optimization techniques are essential for ensuring that SQL Server performs efficiently, especially as your data grows. In this chapter, we covered types of indexes, indexing strategies, query optimization techniques, and the importance of regular index and statistics maintenance. With these skills, you'll be able to design efficient indexing strategies, monitor query performance, and ensure your SQL Server databases can handle complex queries with minimal latency. In the next chapter, we'll explore stored procedures and functions, which can further enhance your SQL Server capabilities by encapsulating complex logic and reusing code effectively.

CHAPTER 9: STORED PROCEDURES AND FUNCTIONS

Overview

Stored procedures and functions are essential tools in SQL Server for encapsulating complex logic, improving code reusability, and optimizing performance. By grouping SQL statements into named blocks of code, stored procedures and functions allow for modular, reusable, and maintainable database logic. This chapter covers the basics of creating and using stored procedures and functions, explaining when to use each and how they can improve the efficiency and organization of your SQL Server database.

1. Introduction to Stored Procedures

A **stored procedure** is a precompiled collection of one or more SQL statements that can be executed with a single command. Stored procedures can accept parameters, handle conditional logic, and include transaction management, making them a powerful tool for encapsulating business logic within SQL Server.

Benefits of Stored Procedures:

- **Performance**: Stored procedures are precompiled, reducing the parsing and optimization time for each execution.
- **Code Reusability**: Commonly used queries and operations can be reused without rewriting code.

- **Security**: Stored procedures allow for granular permission control, enabling access to specific operations without exposing table structures.

Syntax:

sql

```
CREATE PROCEDURE procedure_name
    @Parameter1 DATATYPE,
    @Parameter2 DATATYPE = default_value -- Optional
parameter with default value
AS
BEGIN
    -- SQL statements
END;
```

Example: Create a stored procedure to retrieve employee information based on department.

sql

```
CREATE PROCEDURE GetEmployeesByDepartment
    @DepartmentID INT
AS
BEGIN
    SELECT EmployeeID, FirstName, LastName, JobTitle
    FROM Employees
```

  WHERE DepartmentID = @DepartmentID;

END;

Executing the Stored Procedure:

sql

EXEC GetEmployeesByDepartment @DepartmentID = 3;

In this example, the stored procedure GetEmployeesByDepartment accepts a department ID as a parameter and returns employees in that department.

2. Parameters in Stored Procedures

Stored procedures can accept **input parameters** to customize execution, as well as **output parameters** to return values.

Example of Output Parameter: Create a procedure that calculates the total salary of a department.

sql

```
CREATE PROCEDURE GetTotalSalaryByDepartment
    @DepartmentID INT,
    @TotalSalary DECIMAL(18, 2) OUTPUT
AS
BEGIN
    SELECT @TotalSalary = SUM(Salary)
    FROM Employees
    WHERE DepartmentID = @DepartmentID;
END;
```

Executing with Output Parameter:

sql

```
DECLARE @TotalSalary DECIMAL(18, 2);
EXEC GetTotalSalaryByDepartment @DepartmentID = 3,
@TotalSalary = @TotalSalary OUTPUT;
SELECT @TotalSalary AS TotalSalary;
```

In this example, the procedure calculates the total salary for a given department and returns it through the @TotalSalary output parameter.

3. Conditional Logic and Flow Control in Stored Procedures

Stored procedures support control-of-flow statements like IF, ELSE, WHILE, and BEGIN...END blocks, allowing for conditional logic and looping.

Example: Use conditional logic to give a salary bonus to employees in a specific department.

sql

```
CREATE PROCEDURE GiveDepartmentBonus
    @DepartmentID INT,
    @BonusAmount DECIMAL(10, 2)
AS
BEGIN
    IF @BonusAmount > 0
    BEGIN
```

```
    UPDATE Employees

    SET Salary = Salary + @BonusAmount

    WHERE DepartmentID = @DepartmentID;

END

ELSE

BEGIN

    PRINT 'Bonus amount must be greater than zero.';

END

END;
```

In this procedure, an IF statement checks whether the bonus amount is positive before updating salaries.

4. Error Handling in Stored Procedures

Error handling within stored procedures can be managed using TRY...CATCH blocks, allowing you to handle errors gracefully and return error information if needed.

Example: Error handling in a stored procedure that transfers funds between accounts.

```sql
sql
CREATE PROCEDURE TransferFunds
    @FromAccountID INT,
    @ToAccountID INT,
    @Amount DECIMAL(10, 2)
AS
BEGIN
```

```
BEGIN TRY
    BEGIN TRANSACTION;

    -- Subtract from the source account
    UPDATE Accounts
    SET Balance = Balance - @Amount
    WHERE AccountID = @FromAccountID;

    -- Add to the destination account
    UPDATE Accounts
    SET Balance = Balance + @Amount
    WHERE AccountID = @ToAccountID;

    COMMIT TRANSACTION;
END TRY
BEGIN CATCH
    ROLLBACK TRANSACTION;
    PRINT 'An error occurred: ' + ERROR_MESSAGE();
END CATCH;
END;
```

In this example, a TRY...CATCH block handles potential errors during a funds transfer. If any error occurs, the transaction rolls back, ensuring data integrity.

5. Introduction to Functions

A **function** is a special SQL Server object that performs a calculation and returns a single value or a table. Unlike stored procedures, functions cannot change database state (no INSERT, UPDATE, or DELETE operations). Functions are ideal for calculations or transformations that can be reused in queries.

Types of Functions:

- **Scalar Functions**: Returns a single value, such as an integer or string.
- **Table-Valued Functions (TVFs)**: Returns a table result set.

Syntax for Scalar Function:

```sql
CREATE FUNCTION function_name (@Parameter DATATYPE)
RETURNS DATATYPE
AS
BEGIN
   -- Logic
   RETURN value;
END;
```

Example of Scalar Function: Calculate the age of an employee based on their date of birth.

```sql
CREATE FUNCTION CalculateAge (@BirthDate DATE)
```

```
RETURNS INT
AS
BEGIN
   RETURN DATEDIFF(YEAR, @BirthDate, GETDATE());
END;
```

Using the Function:

```sql
SELECT FirstName, LastName, dbo.CalculateAge(DateOfBirth)
AS Age
FROM Employees;
```

---

6. Table-Valued Functions (TVFs)

Table-Valued Functions return tables, making them useful for encapsulating complex queries that can be used like views. TVFs can be either **inline** or **multi-statement**.

Syntax for Inline Table-Valued Function:

```sql
CREATE FUNCTION function_name (@Parameter DATATYPE)
RETURNS TABLE
AS
RETURN (
   -- Query returning table
);
```

Example of Inline TVF: Retrieve active employees in a specific department.

sql

```
CREATE FUNCTION GetActiveEmployees (@DepartmentID INT)
RETURNS TABLE
AS
RETURN (
    SELECT EmployeeID, FirstName, LastName
    FROM Employees
    WHERE DepartmentID = @DepartmentID AND IsActive = 1
);
```

Using the Inline TVF:

sql

```
SELECT * FROM dbo.GetActiveEmployees(3);
```

In this example, the TVF GetActiveEmployees filters active employees based on the department and returns the result as a table.

7. Using Functions in Queries

Functions can be used directly in queries to perform calculations, transformations, or data retrievals.

Example: Using a scalar function to format employee names.

sql

Copy code

```
CREATE    FUNCTION    FormatName    (@FirstName
NVARCHAR(50), @LastName NVARCHAR(50))
RETURNS NVARCHAR(100)
AS
BEGIN
   RETURN @LastName + ', ' + @FirstName;
END;
```

Using the Function:

sql

```
SELECT dbo.FormatName(FirstName, LastName) AS FullName
FROM Employees;
```

This function, FormatName, concatenates last name and first name in a formatted way, simplifying repeated formatting logic.

8. Benefits of Using Stored Procedures and Functions

Stored procedures and functions offer several advantages for code maintenance, performance, and security:

- **Encapsulation of Logic**: Encapsulate business logic within the database to promote consistency.
- **Improved Performance**: Stored procedures are precompiled, and functions allow SQL Server to reuse execution plans.
- **Security and Permissions**: Limit access to specific operations and prevent direct access to underlying tables.

- **Reusability and Modularity**: Code can be reused across applications, and changes only need to be made in one place.

9. Best Practices for Stored Procedures and Functions

To maximize the efficiency of stored procedures and functions, follow these best practices:

- **Minimize Logic in Scalar Functions**: Scalar functions in SELECT statements can be slow. Use inline TVFs or other methods if possible.
- **Avoid Cursors in Stored Procedures**: Cursors can be resource-intensive. Use set-based operations whenever possible.
- **Use Parameters Wisely**: Avoid optional parameters in high-performance scenarios, as they can hinder optimization.
- **Avoid Using Functions in WHERE Clauses**: Using functions in WHERE clauses prevents SQL Server from using indexes effectively.
- **Document Your Code**: Add comments to clarify complex logic, making stored procedures and functions easier to understand and maintain.

10. Differences Between Stored Procedures and Functions

While both stored procedures and functions encapsulate SQL logic, they serve different purposes:

Feature	Stored Procedure	Function
Return Value	Returns multiple values or result sets	Returns a single value or table
Data Modification	Can modify data	Cannot modify data
Execution in Queries	Cannot be used in SELECT statements	Can be used in SELECT, WHERE, JOIN
Transaction Support	Supports transactions	Does not support transactions
Caching and Optimization	Precompiled, optimized execution	Execution plan can be reused

Stored procedures are best for complex, multi-step processes, while functions are ideal for reusable calculations or transformations within queries.

Stored procedures and functions are powerful tools for encapsulating logic, improving performance, and maintaining security in SQL Server databases. In this chapter, we explored how to create and use stored procedures and functions, handle parameters, implement conditional logic, and use error handling. By leveraging these tools, you can build modular, reusable, and efficient database logic that enhances the overall structure and functionality of your

SQL Server environment. The next chapter will cover triggers and automated tasks, providing you with further tools for managing database events and ensuring data integrity.

CHAPTER 10: TRIGGERS AND AUTOMATED TASKS

Overview

Triggers and automated tasks play a significant role in maintaining data integrity, automating routine processes, and enforcing business rules in SQL Server. **Triggers** are specialized stored procedures that automatically execute in response to specific events, such as data modifications. **Automated tasks** in SQL Server are typically managed using SQL Server Agent, allowing you to schedule regular jobs like backups, maintenance, and alerts. This chapter will guide you through creating and using triggers, setting up automated tasks, and understanding best practices for each.

1. Introduction to Triggers

A **trigger** is a type of stored procedure that automatically runs when a specified event occurs on a table or view. Triggers can be used to enforce constraints, validate data, log changes, or prevent unauthorized modifications.

Types of Triggers:

- **DML Triggers**: Execute in response to INSERT, UPDATE, or DELETE operations.

- **DDL Triggers**: Fire in response to Data Definition Language (DDL) events like CREATE, ALTER, or DROP statements.
- **Logon Triggers**: Fire when a user session is established in SQL Server, often used for auditing purposes.

2. Creating DML Triggers

DML Triggers are the most commonly used triggers and respond to changes in table data, such as inserts, updates, and deletions.

Syntax:

```sql
CREATE TRIGGER trigger_name
ON table_name
AFTER | INSTEAD OF [INSERT, UPDATE, DELETE]
AS
BEGIN
   -- Trigger logic
END;
```

Example of an AFTER Trigger: Log all updates to an Employees table in an audit table.

```sql
CREATE TABLE EmployeeAudit (
    AuditID INT IDENTITY(1,1) PRIMARY KEY,
    EmployeeID INT,
```

```
OldSalary DECIMAL(10,2),
NewSalary DECIMAL(10,2),
ModifiedDate DATETIME DEFAULT GETDATE()
);


CREATE TRIGGER trg_AuditEmployeeSalaryChange
ON Employees
AFTER UPDATE
AS
BEGIN
  IF UPDATE(Salary)
  BEGIN
    INSERT INTO EmployeeAudit (EmployeeID, OldSalary, NewSalary)
    SELECT i.EmployeeID, d.Salary, i.Salary
    FROM inserted AS i
    JOIN deleted AS d ON i.EmployeeID = d.EmployeeID;
  END
END;
```

In this example, trg_AuditEmployeeSalaryChange fires after any UPDATE on the Employees table. When the Salary column is updated, the old and new values are logged in the EmployeeAudit table.

3. INSTEAD OF Triggers

INSTEAD OF triggers allow you to override the default behavior of INSERT, UPDATE, or DELETE operations. They are commonly used in views to make non-updatable views act like tables.

Example of an INSTEAD OF Trigger: Prevent deletion of records in the Employees table if the employee has pending tasks.

```sql
CREATE TRIGGER trg_PreventDeleteIfTasksPending
ON Employees
INSTEAD OF DELETE
AS
BEGIN
  IF EXISTS (
    SELECT 1 FROM Tasks
    WHERE Tasks.EmployeeID IN (SELECT EmployeeID
FROM deleted) AND Tasks.Status = 'Pending'
  )
  BEGIN
    RAISERROR('Cannot delete employees with pending tasks.',
16, 1);
  END
  ELSE
  BEGIN
    DELETE FROM Employees WHERE EmployeeID IN
(SELECT EmployeeID FROM deleted);
```

```
END
END;
```

This trigger checks if an employee being deleted has any pending tasks. If so, the delete operation is blocked, and an error message is raised. If not, the employee record is deleted as usual.

4. DDL Triggers

DDL Triggers respond to changes in the database schema, such as creating or dropping tables or altering stored procedures. They are useful for enforcing database policies and auditing schema changes.

Example of a DDL Trigger: Log changes to any table structure in the database.

sql

Copy code

```
CREATE TABLE SchemaChangeLog (
    EventID INT IDENTITY(1,1) PRIMARY KEY,
    EventType NVARCHAR(100),
    ObjectName NVARCHAR(100),
    EventTime DATETIME DEFAULT GETDATE()
);


CREATE TRIGGER trg_LogSchemaChanges
ON DATABASE
FOR CREATE_TABLE, ALTER_TABLE, DROP_TABLE
AS
```

BEGIN

   INSERT INTO SchemaChangeLog (EventType, ObjectName)

   VALUES

(EVENTDATA().value('(/EVENT_INSTANCE/EventType)[1]',

'NVARCHAR(100)'),

EVENTDATA().value('(/EVENT_INSTANCE/ObjectName)[1]',

'NVARCHAR(100)'));

END;

In this example, the trg_LogSchemaChanges trigger logs CREATE_TABLE, ALTER_TABLE, and DROP_TABLE events to the SchemaChangeLog table, recording schema changes.

5. Logon Triggers

Logon Triggers execute in response to a user logging into SQL Server, often used for auditing logins, restricting access, or setting session-level configurations.

Example of a Logon Trigger: Limit access to the database during off-hours.

sql

```
CREATE TRIGGER trg_LimitLogonHours
ON ALL SERVER
FOR LOGON
AS
```

```
BEGIN
    DECLARE @Hour INT;
    SET @Hour = DATEPART(HOUR, GETDATE());

    IF @Hour < 9 OR @Hour > 17
    BEGIN
      ROLLBACK;
      PRINT 'Logons are not allowed outside of business hours (9
AM to 5 PM).';
    END
END;
```

This logon trigger prevents users from logging in outside of business hours. The ROLLBACK statement cancels the login attempt, enforcing the rule.

6. Best Practices for Using Triggers

While triggers are powerful, they can lead to complexity and performance issues if not used carefully. Here are some best practices:

- **Limit Trigger Complexity**: Avoid complex logic or extensive calculations within triggers, as they run synchronously with the triggering event and can slow down operations.

- **Avoid Cascading Triggers**: Avoid creating multiple triggers that call each other, as this can lead to infinite loops or excessive resource usage.

- **Use Triggers Judiciously**: Triggers are suitable for enforcing data integrity and auditing but should not replace application logic or workflow automation.

- **Document Trigger Logic**: Document triggers and their purpose, as they can make it harder to track data changes and troubleshoot issues.

7. Introduction to Automated Tasks with SQL Server Agent

SQL Server Agent is a service that automates routine tasks, such as backups, maintenance, and notifications. SQL Server Agent jobs can be scheduled to run at specific times, making it easier to manage maintenance tasks consistently.

Common SQL Server Agent Jobs:

- **Database Backups**: Regularly back up databases to ensure data recovery.

- **Index Maintenance**: Rebuild or reorganize indexes to prevent fragmentation.

- **Data Purging**: Remove outdated data from tables to maintain optimal performance.

- **Alerts and Notifications**: Send alerts based on specific conditions, such as low disk space or failed jobs.

8. Creating and Scheduling SQL Server Agent Jobs

SQL Server Agent jobs consist of **steps** and **schedules**. Each step defines an action, such as executing a stored procedure or a T-SQL command, while the schedule defines when the job runs.

Creating a SQL Server Agent Job:

1. In SQL Server Management Studio (SSMS), expand **SQL Server Agent** and right-click **Jobs,** then select **New Job**.
2. In the **New Job** window, provide a name and description for the job.
3. Define **Job Steps** by specifying actions, such as executing a T-SQL script.
4. Set up a **Schedule** to define when the job runs (e.g., daily, weekly).
5. Configure **Notifications** to send alerts if the job succeeds, fails, or completes.

Example: Create a job to back up the Sales database every day at midnight.

1. **Job Name**: DailySalesBackup
2. **Job Step**:
   o Command: BACKUP DATABASE Sales TO DISK = 'D:\Backups\Sales.bak'
3. **Schedule**:
   o Frequency: Daily

o   Time: 00:00 (midnight)

This job will automatically back up the Sales database daily, ensuring regular data protection.

9. Alerts and Notifications with SQL Server Agent

SQL Server Agent allows you to configure **alerts** that notify administrators of specific events, such as job failures or server performance issues. Alerts can be set to trigger based on various conditions, including error severity levels, SQL Server events, and performance conditions.

Example of Setting Up an Alert:

1. In SSMS, expand **SQL Server Agent** and right-click **Alerts**, then select **New Alert**.
2. Name the alert and select **Type** (e.g., SQL Server Event Alert).
3. Define the alert criteria, such as severity level (e.g., severity 17 for insufficient resources).
4. Set **Response** options, such as notifying an operator via email.

Example: Set up an alert to notify when the server encounters resource errors (severity 17).

With this alert configured, SQL Server Agent will notify the specified operator when a resource error occurs, allowing for quick troubleshooting and response.

10. Maintenance Plans for Automated Database Maintenance

SQL Server **Maintenance Plans** are predefined workflows that automate essential tasks like backups, database integrity checks, and index maintenance. Maintenance Plans simplify complex operations without requiring advanced scripting.

Creating a Maintenance Plan:

1. In SSMS, expand **Management**, right-click **Maintenance Plans**, and select **New Maintenance Plan**.
2. Name the plan and add tasks like **Back Up Database (Full)**, **Rebuild Index**, or **Check Database Integrity**.
3. Set schedules for each task, such as weekly index maintenance or daily backups.
4. Configure notifications to alert administrators in case of task failure.

Maintenance Plans streamline database management, ensuring that routine tasks run consistently with minimal manual intervention.

11. Best Practices for SQL Server Agent Jobs and Automated Tasks

To make the most of automated tasks, follow these best practices:

- **Schedule Jobs During Off-Peak Hours**: Run backups and maintenance tasks during times of low user activity to minimize impact.

- **Monitor Job Performance**: Regularly review job logs and monitor performance to ensure tasks are completed successfully and on time.

- **Use Alerts for Critical Conditions**: Set up alerts for issues that require immediate attention, such as job failures or disk space issues.

- **Document Automation Processes**: Maintain clear documentation of job schedules, maintenance plans, and alert configurations to facilitate troubleshooting and knowledge transfer.

Triggers and automated tasks are invaluable tools for enforcing data integrity, automating routine maintenance, and ensuring database reliability in SQL Server. This chapter covered the essentials of using triggers for event-driven automation and SQL Server Agent for scheduled jobs, along with best practices for maintaining an efficient and well-organized database environment. With these tools in place, you can ensure that your SQL Server instances remain consistent, secure, and responsive to operational needs. In the next chapter, we'll explore views, creating logical layers over tables to simplify data access and enforce data security.

CHAPTER 11: VIEWS: CREATING LOGICAL LAYERS

Overview

In SQL Server, **views** are virtual tables that provide an abstraction layer over the underlying data. Views allow you to simplify complex queries, improve data security, and create reusable query structures that can be used by applications and users without directly exposing the underlying table structures. In this chapter, we'll explore how views work, how to create and manage them, and the various benefits they offer in designing efficient and secure database applications.

1. What is a View?

A **view** is a saved SQL query that presents data from one or more tables as a virtual table. Unlike actual tables, views don't store data themselves; instead, they store the SQL logic that retrieves data from tables. When you query a view, SQL Server dynamically executes the underlying query and returns the result.

Advantages of Views:

- **Data Abstraction**: Hide complex joins and calculations, presenting a simplified version of data.
- **Security**: Restrict access to sensitive columns by exposing only necessary fields.

- **Reusability**: Define reusable query logic that can be called multiple times.
- **Consistency**: Ensure a consistent data format and structure for applications and users.

2. Creating Basic Views

A view is created using the CREATE VIEW statement, followed by a SELECT query that defines the data structure for the view. Once created, a view can be queried just like a table.

Syntax:

sql

```
CREATE VIEW view_name AS
SELECT column1, column2, ...
FROM table_name
WHERE condition;
```

Example: Create a view that shows only active employees' names and departments.

sql

```
CREATE VIEW ActiveEmployees AS
SELECT EmployeeID, FirstName, LastName, Department
FROM Employees
WHERE IsActive = 1;
```

Using the View:

sql

SELECT * FROM ActiveEmployees;

In this example, ActiveEmployees presents a simplified version of the Employees table, showing only active employees without exposing the entire table.

3. Using Views for Data Security and Access Control

Views can be used to restrict access to sensitive data by exposing only specific columns. By granting permissions on views instead of tables, you can control what users see and access.

Example: Create a view that hides salary information in the Employees table.

```sql
Copy code
CREATE VIEW PublicEmployeeInfo AS
SELECT EmployeeID, FirstName, LastName, Department
FROM Employees;
```

In this example, PublicEmployeeInfo excludes salary data, allowing access to basic employee information without exposing sensitive salary details. You can then grant SELECT permissions on the view rather than the entire Employees table to control data access.

4. Simplifying Complex Queries with Views

Views can simplify complex queries by encapsulating logic like joins, subqueries, and aggregations. By creating a view, you can reuse the query logic without rewriting it, making code cleaner and easier to maintain.

Example: Create a view that shows total sales by customer.

sql

```
CREATE VIEW CustomerSalesSummary AS
SELECT c.CustomerID, c.CustomerName, SUM(o.OrderAmount)
AS TotalSales
FROM Customers c
JOIN Orders o ON c.CustomerID = o.CustomerID
GROUP BY c.CustomerID, c.CustomerName;
```

Using the View:

sql

```
SELECT * FROM CustomerSalesSummary;
```

In this example, CustomerSalesSummary aggregates sales data by customer, allowing users to view summary data without writing complex joins and GROUP BY statements.

5. Updating Data Through Views

SQL Server allows **updatable views**, meaning you can insert, update, or delete data through a view as long as certain conditions are met:

- The view must reference only one table.

- The view cannot include GROUP BY, DISTINCT, JOIN, aggregate functions, or other clauses that alter the row structure.

Example of an Updatable View:

sql

```
CREATE VIEW EmployeeContactInfo AS
SELECT EmployeeID, FirstName, LastName, Email, PhoneNumber
FROM Employees;
```

Updating Data via the View:

sql

```
UPDATE EmployeeContactInfo
SET PhoneNumber = '555-1234'
WHERE EmployeeID = 101;
```

In this example, the EmployeeContactInfo view allows updating of the PhoneNumber column in the underlying Employees table.

6. Using INSTEAD OF Triggers on Views

For views that include complex logic or joins, direct updates aren't possible. However, you can use an **INSTEAD OF trigger** to allow data modification through a view by defining custom logic to handle INSERT, UPDATE, or DELETE operations.

Example: Enable updates on a view that joins Orders and OrderDetails.

```sql
CREATE VIEW OrderSummary AS
SELECT o.OrderID, o.OrderDate, d.ProductID, d.Quantity
FROM Orders o
JOIN OrderDetails d ON o.OrderID = d.OrderID;

CREATE TRIGGER trg_UpdateOrderSummary
ON OrderSummary
INSTEAD OF UPDATE
AS
BEGIN
    UPDATE OrderDetails
    SET Quantity = inserted.Quantity
    FROM inserted
    WHERE OrderDetails.OrderID = inserted.OrderID AND
OrderDetails.ProductID = inserted.ProductID;
END;
```

In this example, the trg_UpdateOrderSummary trigger allows updates to the Quantity column in OrderDetails through the OrderSummary view.

7. Indexed Views for Performance Optimization

SQL Server supports **indexed views**, which store the result set of the view on disk, similar to a materialized view. Indexed views improve performance for frequently accessed, complex queries, but they also require more storage and maintenance.

Requirements for Indexed Views:

- The view must be **schema-bound**.
- The view cannot contain certain elements like subqueries, outer joins, UNION, or aggregate functions.

Creating an Indexed View:

sql

CREATE VIEW SalesSummary

WITH SCHEMABINDING AS

SELECT CustomerID, SUM(OrderAmount) AS TotalSales

FROM dbo.Orders

GROUP BY CustomerID;

CREATE UNIQUE CLUSTERED INDEX idx_SalesSummary ON SalesSummary (CustomerID);

In this example, SalesSummary is a schema-bound view that calculates total sales per customer. The indexed view improves performance for queries against total sales by storing the aggregated results.

8. Partitioned Views for Distributed Data

Partitioned views combine data from multiple tables (often on different servers) into a single logical view, making it appear as if all data is in a single table. Partitioned views are often used for data distribution across multiple databases or servers to improve performance and scalability.

Example of a Partitioned View: Create a view that combines sales data from multiple regional tables.

```sql
CREATE VIEW AllRegionsSales AS
SELECT * FROM Sales_North
UNION ALL
SELECT * FROM Sales_South
UNION ALL
SELECT * FROM Sales_East
UNION ALL
SELECT * FROM Sales_West;
```

In this example, AllRegionsSales combines data from regional sales tables, allowing users to query data across all regions as if it were in a single table.

9. Managing and Modifying Views

To manage views effectively, SQL Server provides options for modifying, renaming, and dropping views.

Modifying a View: Use the ALTER VIEW statement to modify an existing view.

```sql
ALTER VIEW ActiveEmployees AS
```

SELECT EmployeeID, FirstName, LastName, Department, HireDate
FROM Employees
WHERE IsActive = 1;

Renaming a View: Use sp_rename to change the name of an existing view.

sql

EXEC sp_rename 'OldViewName', 'NewViewName';

Dropping a View: Use the DROP VIEW statement to remove a view.

sql

DROP VIEW ActiveEmployees;

10. Best Practices for Using Views

When designing and using views, follow these best practices to maximize performance and maintainability:

- **Keep Views Simple**: Avoid unnecessary joins or complex logic, as views execute every time they are queried. Use views only for relevant data and keep queries optimized.
- **Use Indexed Views Judiciously**: Indexed views improve performance but require additional storage and maintenance. Only create them for views used frequently in performance-critical applications.

- **Name Views Meaningfully**: Name views descriptively to indicate their purpose, such as CustomerSalesSummary or ActiveEmployees.

- **Use Schema-Binding for Consistency**: Schema-binding ensures that changes to the underlying tables don't break the view, providing consistency and reliability.

- **Grant Permissions on Views, Not Tables**: For security purposes, grant users permissions on views rather than directly on the underlying tables, reducing exposure to sensitive data.

- **Avoid Using Views for Frequent Data Modifications**: While views can sometimes support data modifications, they are best suited for read-heavy scenarios.

11. Performance Considerations with Views

While views are powerful, they can impact performance if used incorrectly:

- **Execution Time**: Views execute each time they're called, so complex views can slow down query performance. Consider indexed views if the view is queried frequently.

- **Nested Views**: Avoid chaining views within views, as it complicates execution plans and can significantly reduce performance.

- **Materializing Views with Temporary Tables**: For very complex views, consider materializing the results with a temporary table or indexed view if real-time updates are not required.

Example: Instead of a deeply nested view, materialize the results into a temporary table for better performance.

sql
```
SELECT * INTO #TempSalesSummary FROM CustomerSalesSummary;
```
This approach allows you to optimize performance by executing the query only once and reusing the results.

Views in SQL Server provide a flexible way to create logical layers over your data, offering benefits in data abstraction, security, and query simplification. This chapter covered creating and managing views, using them to enforce access control, and improving performance with indexed and partitioned views. By following best practices and carefully considering performance implications, views can become a powerful tool in your SQL Server toolkit. In the next chapter, we'll discuss transactions and concurrency control, which are crucial for ensuring data consistency and integrity in multi-user environments.

CHAPTER 12: TRANSACTIONS AND CONCURRENCY CONTROL

Overview

Transactions and concurrency control are essential concepts in SQL Server for ensuring data consistency, reliability, and integrity in multi-user environments. A **transaction** is a sequence of operations that are executed as a single unit of work, while **concurrency control** manages how multiple transactions interact with shared data. In this chapter, we'll cover the basics of transactions, transaction isolation levels, and concurrency control techniques in SQL Server to help you manage data access in multi-user scenarios effectively.

1. Understanding Transactions

A **transaction** is a group of one or more SQL statements that execute together as a single unit. If all statements within the transaction succeed, the transaction is **committed**, making the changes permanent. If any statement fails, the transaction is **rolled back**, undoing all changes to maintain data integrity.

ACID Properties of Transactions:

1. **Atomicity**: All parts of a transaction are completed, or none are.
2. **Consistency**: Transactions bring the database from one valid state to another.

3. **Isolation**: Transactions operate independently without interference.

4. **Durability**: Once a transaction is committed, changes are permanent.

Basic Transaction Syntax:

sql

Copy code

```
BEGIN TRANSACTION;
    -- SQL statements
COMMIT; -- or ROLLBACK if needed
```

Example of a Transaction: Transfer funds between two accounts.

sql

```
BEGIN TRANSACTION;


-- Deduct from the source account
UPDATE Accounts
SET Balance = Balance - 100
WHERE AccountID = 1;


-- Add to the destination account
UPDATE Accounts
SET Balance = Balance + 100
WHERE AccountID = 2;
```

COMMIT;

In this example, both updates either complete successfully (commit) or fail together (rollback), ensuring the integrity of the fund transfer.

2. Transaction Control Commands

SQL Server provides three primary commands for managing transactions:

- **BEGIN TRANSACTION**: Starts a new transaction.
- **COMMIT**: Saves changes made within the transaction permanently.
- **ROLLBACK**: Reverts all changes made within the transaction.

Example with Error Handling:

```sql
BEGIN TRANSACTION;

BEGIN TRY
    -- Update statements
    UPDATE Accounts SET Balance = Balance - 100 WHERE AccountID = 1;
    UPDATE Accounts SET Balance = Balance + 100 WHERE AccountID = 2;
```

COMMIT;

END TRY

BEGIN CATCH

ROLLBACK;

PRINT 'Transaction failed: ' + ERROR_MESSAGE();

END CATCH;

Here, if an error occurs, the CATCH block rolls back the transaction to prevent incomplete or inconsistent changes.

3. Isolation Levels in SQL Server

Isolation levels define the degree to which one transaction must be isolated from data modifications made by other transactions. SQL Server supports several isolation levels, each balancing consistency and concurrency differently:

1. **Read Uncommitted**: Allows reading uncommitted data (dirty reads). Fast but prone to inconsistencies.
2. **Read Committed**: Prevents dirty reads by only reading committed data. Default isolation level in SQL Server.
3. **Repeatable Read**: Prevents dirty and non-repeatable reads by holding locks on read rows until the transaction completes.
4. **Serializable**: Highest isolation level, preventing dirty reads, non-repeatable reads, and phantom reads by locking the entire range of data accessed.

5. **Snapshot**: Provides a stable snapshot of data as it was at the start of the transaction, allowing consistent reads without locking other transactions.

Setting Isolation Levels:

sql
SET TRANSACTION ISOLATION LEVEL SERIALIZABLE;

BEGIN TRANSACTION;
-- SQL statements
COMMIT;

Example Use Case: Use READ COMMITTED for quick, safe reads with minimal locking and SERIALIZABLE for scenarios requiring maximum consistency, such as financial transactions.

4. Concurrency Problems and Solutions

Concurrency problems arise when multiple transactions access the same data simultaneously, leading to potential conflicts. Common concurrency issues include:

- **Dirty Reads**: A transaction reads data modified by another transaction that hasn't been committed.
- **Non-Repeatable Reads**: A transaction reads the same data twice but gets different values due to another transaction's update.

- **Phantom Reads**: A transaction reads a set of rows but gets different results in subsequent reads because another transaction inserted or deleted rows.

Examples of Concurrency Solutions:

1. **Using Isolation Levels**: Control the level of data visibility between transactions to avoid concurrency issues.
2. **Optimistic Concurrency**: Suitable for low-conflict scenarios; transactions operate without locking data but check for conflicts before committing.
3. **Pessimistic Concurrency**: Locks data to prevent conflicts, ideal for high-conflict scenarios but may cause delays for other users.

5. Locking Mechanisms in SQL Server

Locks are fundamental to SQL Server's concurrency control, ensuring data consistency by restricting access to data being read or modified by a transaction. SQL Server uses different types of locks based on the operation and isolation level.

Types of Locks:

- **Shared Locks**: Used for read operations, allowing multiple transactions to read but not modify the data.
- **Exclusive Locks**: Used for write operations, preventing other transactions from reading or writing to the data.

- **Update Locks**: Applied before modifying data to prevent conflicts, especially in scenarios where shared locks may lead to deadlocks.

Lock Granularity:

- **Row-level locks**: Lock individual rows; efficient for fine-grained control.
- **Page-level locks**: Lock a data page (group of rows); balance between row and table locks.
- **Table-level locks**: Lock the entire table; simplest but can restrict access for other users.

Example of Locking in SQL Server:

```sql
SET TRANSACTION ISOLATION LEVEL REPEATABLE READ;
BEGIN TRANSACTION;

SELECT * FROM Orders WHERE OrderID = 1 WITH (UPDLOCK);

-- Further actions
COMMIT;
```

In this example, UPDLOCK (update lock) ensures that the row in Orders is locked for update, preventing other transactions from modifying it until the transaction completes.

6. Deadlocks and Deadlock Prevention

A **deadlock** occurs when two or more transactions hold locks on resources that the other transactions need, causing them to wait indefinitely. SQL Server automatically detects deadlocks and resolves them by terminating one of the transactions.

Example of Deadlock Scenario: Transaction A locks Table1 and tries to access Table2, while Transaction B locks Table2 and tries to access Table1. This can result in a deadlock.

Deadlock Prevention Techniques:

1. **Access Resources in a Consistent Order**: Ensure transactions acquire locks in a predefined sequence to avoid circular locking.
2. **Use Lower Isolation Levels**: Using lower isolation levels, such as READ COMMITTED, can reduce locking.
3. **Keep Transactions Short**: Minimize the number of statements within a transaction and avoid lengthy operations.
4. **Use Locking Hints**: Use hints like ROWLOCK, PAGLOCK, or TABLOCK to control locking behavior based on needs.

7. Using Locking Hints for Fine-Grained Control

SQL Server provides **locking hints** to override the default locking behavior for specific queries, giving you more control over concurrency.

Common Locking Hints:

- **ROWLOCK**: Enforces row-level locking.
- **PAGLOCK**: Enforces page-level locking.
- **TABLOCK**: Locks the entire table for the duration of the operation.
- **NOLOCK**: Allows reading uncommitted data, similar to READ UNCOMMITTED isolation level.
- **XLOCK**: Forces exclusive locks on all resources.

Example of Using Locking Hints:

```sql
SELECT * FROM Orders WITH (ROWLOCK, UPDLOCK)
WHERE OrderID = 1;
```

This example enforces a row-level update lock on the selected Orders row, ensuring fine-grained control while preventing other transactions from updating it.

8. Snapshot Isolation for Optimistic Concurrency

Snapshot Isolation is an optimistic concurrency control technique that provides a stable view of data as it was when the transaction started, allowing for consistent reads without blocking other transactions. Snapshot Isolation is beneficial for applications with high read concurrency and low conflict rates.

Enabling Snapshot Isolation:

sql

ALTER   DATABASE   YourDatabase   SET ALLOW_SNAPSHOT_ISOLATION ON;

Using Snapshot Isolation:

sql

SET TRANSACTION ISOLATION LEVEL SNAPSHOT;

BEGIN TRANSACTION;

-- Operations

COMMIT;

Snapshot Isolation eliminates most locking issues by providing a versioned view of data, reducing contention between read and write operations.

9. Best Practices for Transaction Management

To ensure effective transaction management and avoid concurrency issues, follow these best practices:

- **Keep Transactions Short**: Limit transactions to essential operations only, reducing the duration of locks and improving concurrency.

- **Use Appropriate Isolation Levels**: Choose isolation levels based on the need for data consistency and concurrency.

- **Avoid Long-Running Transactions**: Long-running transactions can hold locks and cause contention. Break up complex operations when possible.

- **Handle Errors Gracefully**: Use TRY...CATCH blocks to handle transaction errors and avoid partial updates.

- **Regularly Monitor Locks and Deadlocks**: Use SQL Server's dynamic management views (DMVs) to monitor lock usage and identify deadlock patterns.

10. Monitoring and Troubleshooting Concurrency with Dynamic Management Views

SQL Server provides several Dynamic Management Views (DMVs) for monitoring transactions, locks, and deadlocks, helping you identify and troubleshoot concurrency issues.

Key DMVs:

- **sys.dm_tran_locks**: Shows details of active locks in the system.

- **sys.dm_exec_requests**: Provides information on currently executing requests, including wait times and blocking.

- **sys.dm_os_waiting_tasks**: Lists tasks waiting on resources, useful for identifying blocking and deadlocks.

Example of Monitoring Locks:

sql

```
SELECT          resource_type,          resource_associated_entity_id,
request_mode, request_status
FROM sys.dm_tran_locks;
```

This query provides information about active locks in SQL Server, allowing you to identify which resources are locked and by whom.

Conclusion

Transactions and concurrency control are essential for managing data integrity and consistency in SQL Server, especially in multi-user environments. In this chapter, we covered the fundamentals of transactions, isolation levels, and locking mechanisms, as well as techniques for avoiding concurrency issues like deadlocks. By understanding these concepts and following best practices, you can ensure that your database transactions are safe, efficient, and reliable. In the next chapter, we'll dive into error handling and debugging techniques, which will help you catch and handle issues within your SQL Server code effectively.

CHAPTER 13: ERROR HANDLING AND DEBUGGING

Overview

Error handling and debugging are essential skills in SQL Server development and administration. Effective error handling ensures that your code can manage unexpected situations without disrupting operations, while debugging tools help you identify and resolve issues. In this chapter, we'll explore techniques for error handling, using TRY...CATCH blocks, working with system error functions, and leveraging debugging tools in SQL Server Management Studio (SSMS) to troubleshoot issues.

1. Understanding Error Handling in SQL Server

Error handling in SQL Server involves capturing and responding to unexpected conditions, such as constraint violations, data type mismatches, and connectivity issues. SQL Server provides tools and functions for handling errors gracefully and allows you to log error information for analysis.

Benefits of Error Handling:

- **Data Integrity**: Rollback incomplete transactions to maintain database consistency.
- **User Feedback**: Return informative error messages to users or applications.

- **Logging**: Record error details for debugging and troubleshooting.

2. Using TRY...CATCH for Error Handling

The **TRY...CATCH** construct in SQL Server allows you to handle errors in a controlled manner. Statements within the TRY block are executed as usual, but if an error occurs, control is transferred to the CATCH block.

Basic Syntax:

```sql
BEGIN TRY
    -- Code to execute
END TRY
BEGIN CATCH
    -- Error handling code
END CATCH;
```

Example: Handle errors in a fund transfer transaction.

```sql
BEGIN TRY
    BEGIN TRANSACTION;


    -- Deduct from the source account
    UPDATE Accounts
    SET Balance = Balance - 100
```

```
WHERE AccountID = 1;


-- Add to the destination account
UPDATE Accounts
SET Balance = Balance + 100
WHERE AccountID = 2;


COMMIT;
END TRY
BEGIN CATCH
ROLLBACK;
PRINT 'An error occurred during the transaction: ' +
ERROR_MESSAGE();
END CATCH;
```

In this example, if an error occurs in any UPDATE statement, the transaction is rolled back, and an error message is printed.

3. System Error Functions

SQL Server provides several system error functions that you can use within CATCH blocks to capture details about the error. Key functions include:

- **ERROR_MESSAGE()**: Returns the error message text.
- **ERROR_NUMBER()**: Returns the error number.
- **ERROR_SEVERITY()**: Indicates the error severity level.
- **ERROR_STATE()**: Returns the state of the error.

- **ERROR_LINE()**: Indicates the line number where the error occurred.
- **ERROR_PROCEDURE()**: Returns the name of the stored procedure or trigger where the error occurred.

Example: Use error functions to log error details.

```sql
BEGIN TRY
    -- Sample SQL code
END TRY
BEGIN CATCH
    DECLARE @ErrorMessage NVARCHAR(4000) = ERROR_MESSAGE();
    DECLARE @ErrorSeverity INT = ERROR_SEVERITY();
    DECLARE @ErrorLine INT = ERROR_LINE();

    PRINT 'Error message: ' + @ErrorMessage;
    PRINT 'Error severity: ' + CAST(@ErrorSeverity AS NVARCHAR(10));
    PRINT 'Error occurred on line: ' + CAST(@ErrorLine AS NVARCHAR(10));
END CATCH;
```

This code captures error details and prints them, which can be logged for further investigation.

4. Logging Errors in a Custom Error Log Table

Creating a custom error log table allows you to persist error details for analysis, making it easier to track recurring issues.

Create an Error Log Table:

sql

```
CREATE TABLE ErrorLog (
    ErrorID INT IDENTITY(1,1) PRIMARY KEY,
    ErrorMessage NVARCHAR(4000),
    ErrorSeverity INT,
    ErrorState INT,
    ErrorProcedure NVARCHAR(200),
    ErrorLine INT,
    ErrorDate DATETIME DEFAULT GETDATE()
);
```

Log Errors Using INSERT Statements:

sql

```
BEGIN TRY
    -- Sample SQL code
END TRY
BEGIN CATCH
    INSERT INTO ErrorLog (ErrorMessage, ErrorSeverity, ErrorState, ErrorProcedure, ErrorLine)
    VALUES (
      ERROR_MESSAGE(),
```

```
ERROR_SEVERITY(),
ERROR_STATE(),
ERROR_PROCEDURE(),
ERROR_LINE()
);
END CATCH;
```

In this example, error details are inserted into the ErrorLog table, where you can later review them for troubleshooting purposes.

5. THROW and RAISERROR for Custom Error Messages

SQL Server provides two options for raising errors manually:

- **THROW**: Introduced in SQL Server 2012, THROW is used to raise exceptions. It requires only an error message and automatically rolls back the transaction if it's in progress.
- **RAISERROR**: Allows more customization of error messages, including severity and state, but requires a custom error message or error number.

Using THROW:

sql

```
THROW 50001, 'A custom error occurred.', 1;
```

Using RAISERROR:

sql

RAISERROR('A custom error occurred: %s', 16, 1, 'specific issue details');

Example of RAISERROR with TRY...CATCH:

```sql
BEGIN TRY
   IF @Balance < 0
   BEGIN
      RAISERROR('Balance cannot be negative.', 16, 1);
   END
END TRY
BEGIN CATCH
   PRINT 'Error: ' + ERROR_MESSAGE();
END CATCH;
```

Here, RAISERROR raises an error if @Balance is negative, allowing for custom error handling logic.

6. Debugging with SQL Server Management Studio (SSMS)

SSMS provides several debugging tools that make it easier to step through and examine SQL code.

Enabling Debugging in SSMS: To start debugging, click on **Debug** or press **Alt + F5** in SSMS.

Key Debugging Tools:

- **Breakpoints**: Set breakpoints to pause execution at specific lines of code, allowing you to inspect variable values and flow.

- **Step Over (F10)**: Execute the current line of code without diving into procedures or functions.

- **Step Into (F11)**: Step into procedures or functions to examine code in detail.

- **Locals and Watch Windows**: View the current values of variables and expressions in the Locals or Watch window.

Example of Using Breakpoints: Suppose you're debugging a stored procedure for a fund transfer. Place a breakpoint at the first UPDATE statement to check if values are being updated as expected. Then use the Watch window to observe changes to variables like @Balance.

7. Using PRINT Statements for Simple Debugging

If you can't use the SSMS debugger, PRINT statements are a straightforward alternative to display variable values or indicate the progress of a procedure.

Example with PRINT Statements:

```sql
DECLARE @Counter INT = 0;


WHILE @Counter < 5
```

BEGIN

    PRINT 'Counter is: ' + CAST(@Counter AS NVARCHAR(10));

    SET @Counter = @Counter + 1;

END;

In this example, PRINT outputs the value of @Counter in each loop iteration, which can help you verify that the loop works as intended.

8. Using Dynamic Management Views (DMVs) for Troubleshooting

SQL Server **Dynamic Management Views (DMVs)** provide insights into query performance, resource usage, and error information, making them invaluable for troubleshooting.

Key DMVs for Error Handling and Debugging:

- **sys.dm_exec_query_stats**: Provides execution statistics for cached queries.
- **sys.dm_exec_sessions**: Shows information about active sessions, including error details.
- **sys.dm_tran_locks**: Displays lock details, useful for deadlock analysis.
- **sys.dm_os_waiting_tasks**: Shows tasks waiting for resources, which can help identify blocking issues.

Example: Monitor currently running queries for performance issues.

sql

```
SELECT
    s.session_id,
    r.status,
    r.command,
    r.cpu_time,
    r.total_elapsed_time,
    q.text AS query_text
FROM sys.dm_exec_requests AS r
JOIN sys.dm_exec_sessions AS s ON r.session_id = s.session_id
CROSS APPLY sys.dm_exec_sql_text(r.sql_handle) AS q
WHERE s.is_user_process = 1;
```

This query shows active user processes, helping you identify slow or problematic queries.

9. Error Handling Best Practices

Effective error handling and debugging are essential for building robust SQL Server applications. Follow these best practices:

- **Use TRY...CATCH for Transactions**: Always use TRY...CATCH in transactions to manage unexpected errors and ensure data integrity.
- **Log Errors for Troubleshooting**: Record errors in a log table to identify recurring issues and analyze error patterns.
- **Use THROW Instead of RAISERROR**: Prefer THROW for raising errors in new code, as it's simpler and rolls back transactions automatically.

- **Avoid Suppressing Errors**: Ensure errors are logged or handled, even if they're not shown to end users.
- **Limit Error Handling Logic in the Application Layer**: Use SQL Server's error-handling capabilities instead of relying on application-level error handling.

10. Monitoring and Analyzing Error Patterns

Monitoring error patterns helps you proactively address issues and improve the stability of your SQL Server environment. Common monitoring techniques include:

- **Reviewing the Error Log Table**: Regularly analyze your custom error log table for trends and patterns.
- **Using SQL Server Agent Alerts**: Set up alerts for specific error severities to get immediate notifications of critical issues.
- **Configuring Performance Counters**: Use performance counters to monitor error-related metrics, such as deadlock rate or failed logins.

Example: Set up an alert for all severity 16 errors.

1. In SQL Server Management Studio, go to **SQL Server Agent > Alerts > New Alert**.
2. Set **Name** to "Severity 16 Errors" and **Type** to SQL Server Event Alert.

3. Set **Severity** to 16.

4. Define **Response** options, such as sending an email to the database administrator.

Error handling and debugging are crucial for developing and maintaining stable SQL Server applications. This chapter covered TRY...CATCH blocks, error functions, custom error logging, and SSMS debugging tools, providing you with essential techniques to manage and troubleshoot errors effectively. By implementing robust error-handling practices and monitoring for recurring issues, you can build more resilient SQL Server solutions and improve overall application stability. In the next chapter, we'll dive into SQL Server security essentials, focusing on protecting your data and controlling access to sensitive information.

CHAPTER 14: SQL SERVER SECURITY ESSENTIALS

Overview

Security is a critical aspect of SQL Server management, protecting data from unauthorized access, manipulation, and breaches. SQL Server offers multiple layers of security, including authentication, authorization, and encryption, to ensure that only authorized users can access and manipulate data. In this chapter, we'll explore SQL Server security essentials, covering user authentication, role-based access control, permissions, and encryption strategies to help you safeguard your SQL Server environment.

1. Authentication in SQL Server

Authentication is the process of verifying the identity of a user or application trying to access SQL Server. SQL Server supports two main types of authentication:

1. **Windows Authentication**: Integrates with Active Directory, allowing users to access SQL Server using their Windows credentials. This method is more secure and is recommended for environments where SQL Server is part of a Windows domain.

2. **SQL Server Authentication**: Requires a SQL Server-specific username and password, independent of Windows

credentials. This method is useful for users or applications outside the Windows domain but requires strong password policies to ensure security.

Setting the Authentication Mode:

1. In SQL Server Management Studio (SSMS), right-click on the server, select **Properties**, then go to the **Security** page.
2. Choose **Windows Authentication mode** or **SQL Server and Windows Authentication mode** (Mixed Mode).
3. Restart the SQL Server instance to apply changes.

Example of Creating a SQL Server Login:

sql

Copy code

```
CREATE    LOGIN    sqlUser    WITH    PASSWORD    =
'StrongPassword!@#';
```

In this example, a login named sqlUser is created with a strong password, which will use SQL Server Authentication to access the server.

2. Authorization: Users and Roles

Authorization in SQL Server determines what authenticated users can do within the database. SQL Server offers granular access control through **roles** and **permissions**.

Key Security Roles:

- **Server Roles**: Apply server-wide permissions, such as sysadmin (full control), dbcreator (create databases), and securityadmin (manage logins).
- **Database Roles**: Control access at the database level. SQL Server includes built-in roles like db_owner, db_datareader, and db_datawriter.

Example of Adding a User to a Role:

sql

Copy code

```
USE MyDatabase;
CREATE USER dbUser FOR LOGIN sqlUser;
EXEC sp_addrolemember 'db_datareader', 'dbUser';
```

This example creates a database user dbUser mapped to the login sqlUser and adds it to the db_datareader role, granting read-only access to the database.

3. Granting and Revoking Permissions

SQL Server allows you to grant and revoke specific permissions on database objects (such as tables, views, and stored procedures) using **GRANT** and **REVOKE** statements.

Common Permissions:

- **SELECT**: Read data from a table or view.
- **INSERT**: Insert new data into a table.

- **UPDATE**: Modify existing data in a table.
- **DELETE**: Remove data from a table.
- **EXECUTE**: Run a stored procedure or function.

Granting Permissions:

sql

GRANT SELECT ON Employees TO dbUser;

GRANT EXECUTE ON uspGetEmployeeData TO dbUser;

Revoking Permissions:

sql

Copy code

REVOKE SELECT ON Employees FROM dbUser;

In this example, dbUser is granted the SELECT permission on the Employees table and the EXECUTE permission on a stored procedure. Revoking permissions removes access without affecting other permissions.

4. Role-Based Access Control (RBAC)

Role-Based Access Control (RBAC) simplifies permission management by assigning users to roles with predefined permissions, rather than granting individual permissions to each user. Using roles, you can group users by job function or responsibility, making access control more manageable.

Custom Database Roles: You can create custom database roles to fit specific business needs.

Example of Creating a Custom Role:

sql

USE MyDatabase;

CREATE ROLE SalesRole;

GRANT SELECT, INSERT, UPDATE ON Orders TO SalesRole;

-- Add a user to the custom role

EXEC sp_addrolemember 'SalesRole', 'dbUser';

In this example, SalesRole is a custom role that allows SELECT, INSERT, and UPDATE permissions on the Orders table, which can then be assigned to multiple users.

5. Row-Level Security (RLS)

Row-Level Security (RLS) allows you to control access to individual rows in a table based on the user's characteristics, such as their role or department. RLS is helpful for multi-tenant applications where each user should only see data they are authorized to access.

Implementing Row-Level Security:

1. Create a security predicate function to filter rows.
2. Bind the predicate to a table using a security policy.

Example of Row-Level Security:

sql

```
-- Security Predicate Function
CREATE FUNCTION fn_SalesFilter (@SalesPersonID INT)
RETURNS TABLE
WITH SCHEMABINDING
AS
RETURN SELECT 1 AS Allowed
    WHERE @SalesPersonID = USER_ID();
```

```
-- Security Policy
CREATE SECURITY POLICY SalesPolicy
ADD FILTER PREDICATE fn_SalesFilter(SalesPersonID) ON
Sales;
```

In this example, each salesperson only sees rows in the Sales table where SalesPersonID matches their user ID, enforcing row-level security.

6. Data Encryption

Encryption protects sensitive data by transforming it into an unreadable format for unauthorized users. SQL Server supports both **transparent data encryption (TDE)** and **column-level encryption**.

Transparent Data Encryption (TDE): TDE encrypts the entire database, protecting data at rest. TDE is commonly used to secure backups and prevent unauthorized access to the physical database files.

Enabling TDE:

sql

```
USE master;
CREATE DATABASE ENCRYPTION KEY
WITH ALGORITHM = AES_256;
ALTER DATABASE MyDatabase SET ENCRYPTION ON;
```

Column-Level Encryption: Column-level encryption allows you to encrypt specific columns containing sensitive data, such as Social Security numbers or credit card information.

Example of Column-Level Encryption:

1. Create a symmetric key.
2. Encrypt data using the key.

sql

```
CREATE SYMMETRIC KEY MyKey WITH ALGORITHM =
AES_256 ENCRYPTION BY PASSWORD =
'MyStrongPassword';
OPEN SYMMETRIC KEY MyKey DECRYPTION BY
PASSWORD = 'MyStrongPassword';


-- Encrypt column data
UPDATE Employees
SET EncryptedSSN = ENCRYPTBYKEY(KEY_GUID('MyKey'),
SSN);
```

-- Decrypt data for use

SELECT   SSN   =   CONVERT(NVARCHAR,
DECRYPTBYKEY(EncryptedSSN))

FROM Employees;

CLOSE SYMMETRIC KEY MyKey;

In this example, SSN data in the Employees table is encrypted and decrypted using a symmetric key.

7. Always Encrypted

Always Encrypted allows sensitive data to be encrypted both at rest and in transit, even preventing database administrators from viewing sensitive information. The encryption and decryption occur at the client side, making it ideal for highly secure applications.

Setting Up Always Encrypted:

1. Define encryption keys on the client side.
2. Configure columns as encrypted.

Example: Using Always Encrypted requires configuration in SSMS and the application code to manage encryption keys, making it more complex than TDE but providing stronger security.

8. Auditing and Monitoring

Auditing and monitoring track SQL Server activities to ensure compliance with security policies and detect suspicious behavior. SQL Server provides several tools for auditing and monitoring:

- **SQL Server Audit**: Tracks server and database events, such as login attempts and data access, and logs them to an audit file or the Windows Security log.
- **Dynamic Management Views (DMVs)**: Show real-time information about sessions, permissions, and query execution.
- **Extended Events**: Lightweight event-tracking system for monitoring detailed database activities.

Creating a SQL Server Audit:

```sql
-- Create the audit object
CREATE SERVER AUDIT MyAudit
TO FILE (FILEPATH = 'C:\AuditLogs\MyAuditLog.sqlaudit');


-- Define the audit action
CREATE DATABASE AUDIT SPECIFICATION MyDatabaseAuditSpec
FOR SERVER AUDIT MyAudit
ADD (SELECT ON OBJECT::Employees BY dbUser);
```

-- Enable the audit

ALTER SERVER AUDIT MyAudit WITH (STATE = ON);

ALTER DATABASE AUDIT SPECIFICATION MyDatabaseAuditSpec WITH (STATE = ON);

This example audits SELECT operations on the Employees table by dbUser and logs them in MyAuditLog.sqlaudit.

9. Best Practices for SQL Server Security

Following security best practices ensures a secure SQL Server environment:

- **Use Windows Authentication Whenever Possible**: Rely on Windows Authentication for stronger security and ease of management.
- **Enforce Strong Password Policies**: For SQL Server Authentication, enforce complex passwords and regular password changes.
- **Implement Principle of Least Privilege**: Grant only the necessary permissions and avoid using high-privilege roles like sysadmin for regular operations.
- **Use Row-Level Security (RLS) for Multi-Tenant Environments**: Limit data access at the row level for users in multi-tenant applications.
- **Regularly Review Permissions**: Periodically review and audit user permissions to identify and remove any unnecessary privileges.

- **Enable Encryption for Sensitive Data**: Use TDE for database encryption and column-level or Always Encrypted for sensitive data.

- **Monitor and Audit Database Activity**: Use SQL Server Audit and DMVs to monitor activity and detect unauthorized access or suspicious behavior.

10. Monitoring Security with Dynamic Management Views

Dynamic Management Views (DMVs) provide insights into security-related information, including user permissions, active sessions, and failed login attempts.

Example DMVs for Security Monitoring:

- **sys.database_principals**: Shows database users and roles.
- **sys.server_principals**: Displays server logins and roles.
- **sys.dm_exec_sessions**: Lists active sessions, useful for monitoring user activity.
- **sys.dm_exec_connections**: Provides information on current connections, including login details.

Example: Query user permissions using DMVs.

sql

```
SELECT p.name AS UserName, r.name AS RoleName
FROM sys.database_role_members AS m
```

```
JOIN sys.database_principals AS r ON m.role_principal_id =
r.principal_id
JOIN sys.database_principals AS p ON m.member_principal_id =
p.principal_id;
```

This query shows users and their assigned roles in the current database, helping you identify access levels.

Securing SQL Server is essential for protecting data integrity and ensuring compliance with data security regulations. This chapter covered the essentials of SQL Server security, including authentication, authorization, role-based access, encryption, and auditing. By implementing these practices and leveraging SQL Server's security features, you can build a robust security framework that safeguards sensitive information and ensures only authorized users have access to the data they need. In the next chapter, we'll dive into SQL Server backup and recovery strategies, which are crucial for data protection and disaster recovery.

CHAPTER 15: DATA BACKUP AND RECOVERY

Overview

Data backup and recovery are fundamental aspects of SQL Server management, ensuring that your data is protected from accidental deletion, hardware failures, or catastrophic events. SQL Server provides a variety of backup options and recovery models that allow you to restore databases to specific points in time, minimizing data loss. In this chapter, we'll cover SQL Server backup types, recovery models, and best practices for creating an effective backup and recovery strategy.

1. Understanding SQL Server Recovery Models

SQL Server offers three recovery models, each defining how transactions are logged and how backups can be used to restore data. Choosing the right recovery model depends on your data recovery requirements and acceptable levels of data loss.

Recovery Models:

1. **Simple Recovery**: Minimal transaction logging. Suitable for non-critical databases where some data loss is acceptable.
2. **Full Recovery**: All transactions are fully logged, allowing for point-in-time recovery. Ideal for critical databases where data loss is unacceptable.

3. **Bulk-Logged Recovery**: Minimal logging for bulk operations, reducing log space usage while retaining recovery capabilities. This model is a balance between performance and recoverability.

Setting the Recovery Model:

sql

Copy code

ALTER DATABASE MyDatabase SET RECOVERY FULL;

In this example, the MyDatabase database is set to the **Full Recovery** model, enabling point-in-time recovery.

2. Types of Backups in SQL Server

SQL Server offers several types of backups, each serving different purposes. Combining these backup types provides a comprehensive backup and recovery strategy.

Backup Types:

- **Full Backup**: Backs up the entire database, including all data and transaction log entries. This is the foundation of most backup plans.
- **Differential Backup**: Backs up only changes made since the last full backup, saving time and storage space. Differential backups require a recent full backup to restore.

- **Transaction Log Backup**: Backs up the transaction log, capturing all changes since the last log backup. Essential for point-in-time recovery in the Full Recovery model.
- **Copy-Only Backup**: A special full backup that doesn't interfere with the backup sequence, useful for ad-hoc backups.
- **File/Filegroup Backup**: Backs up specific files or filegroups within a database, ideal for very large databases where full backups may be impractical.

Example of a Full Backup:

sql

Copy code

BACKUP DATABASE MyDatabase TO DISK = 'D:\Backups\MyDatabase_Full.bak';

This command creates a full backup of MyDatabase, which can be used as a baseline for future differential and transaction log backups.

. Full Backup: The Foundation of Recovery

A **full backup** is the complete backup of the database and serves as the starting point for differential and transaction log backups. Full backups include all data, system tables, and transaction logs at the time of the backup, making it essential for any recovery plan.

Creating a Full Backup in SQL Server Management Studio (SSMS):

1. In SSMS, right-click on the database, select **Tasks > Back Up**.
2. Choose **Backup Type** as Full.
3. Set the **Destination** (e.g., a local file path or a network location).
4. Click **OK** to start the backup.

It's best practice to perform full backups regularly (e.g., weekly) as part of your backup schedule.

4. *Differential Backup: Saving Only Changes*

A **differential backup** captures only the data changes made since the last full backup, making it smaller and faster than a full backup. Differential backups are cumulative, so each differential backup includes all changes since the last full backup.

Example of a Differential Backup:

sql

Copy code

```
BACKUP DATABASE MyDatabase TO DISK = 'D:\Backups\MyDatabase_Diff.bak' WITH DIFFERENTIAL;
```

Differential backups are usually scheduled more frequently than full backups (e.g., daily) to minimize the time needed for restoration in case of failure.

5. *Transaction Log Backup: Enabling Point-in-Time Recovery*

Transaction log backups capture all transactions that have occurred since the last transaction log backup. In the **Full Recovery** model, transaction log backups are essential for point-in-time recovery.

Example of a Transaction Log Backup:

sql

Copy code

```
BACKUP LOG MyDatabase TO DISK = 'D:\Backups\MyDatabase_Log.trn';
```

Transaction log backups are typically scheduled frequently (e.g., every 15 minutes) to minimize potential data loss.

Restoring to a Specific Point in Time:

1. Restore the last full backup.
2. Restore the latest differential backup (if available).
3. Restore transaction log backups, specifying a point in time if needed.

This allows you to recover the database to a precise moment, providing flexibility in recovery.

6. Backup Compression

SQL Server supports **backup compression** to reduce the size of backup files, saving storage space and potentially speeding up the backup and restore processes. However, backup compression requires more CPU resources, which may impact performance.

Enabling Backup Compression:

sql

Copy code

BACKUP DATABASE MyDatabase TO DISK = 'D:\Backups\MyDatabase_Compressed.bak' WITH COMPRESSION;

You can also configure SQL Server to compress all backups by default:

1. In SSMS, right-click on the server instance and select **Properties**.
2. Go to the **Database Settings** tab and check **Compress Backup**.

7. Restoring Backups

SQL Server provides several restore options, allowing you to recover a database to a specific point in time using full, differential, and transaction log backups.

Basic Restore Syntax:

sql

Copy code

```
RESTORE DATABASE MyDatabase FROM DISK =
'D:\Backups\MyDatabase_Full.bak';
```

Restoring with Differential and Transaction Log Backups:

sql

Copy code

```
RESTORE DATABASE MyDatabase FROM DISK =
'D:\Backups\MyDatabase_Full.bak' WITH NORECOVERY;
RESTORE DATABASE MyDatabase FROM DISK =
'D:\Backups\MyDatabase_Diff.bak' WITH NORECOVERY;
RESTORE LOG MyDatabase FROM DISK =
'D:\Backups\MyDatabase_Log.trn' WITH RECOVERY;
```

In this example, NORECOVERY keeps the database in a restoring state, allowing you to apply subsequent backups. The final WITH RECOVERY statement brings the database online.

8. Implementing a Backup and Restore Strategy

A solid backup strategy balances data protection and performance, ensuring minimal data loss and rapid recovery in the event of a failure.

Example Backup Schedule:

- **Weekly Full Backup**: Every Sunday at midnight.
- **Daily Differential Backup**: Every day at midnight.
- **Frequent Transaction Log Backups**: Every 15 minutes.

Recovery Strategy:

1. Restore the most recent full backup.
2. Apply the latest differential backup (if available).
3. Apply transaction log backups up to the desired recovery point.

This strategy allows you to minimize data loss and downtime, while keeping backup storage requirements manageable.

9. Backup Verification and Monitoring

It's crucial to regularly verify backups to ensure they're complete and usable for restoration.

Verifying Backups:

sql

Copy code

```
RESTORE VERIFYONLY FROM DISK = 'D:\Backups\MyDatabase_Full.bak';
```

This command checks the integrity of the backup file without restoring it. It's best practice to verify backups periodically to avoid unexpected issues during restoration.

Automating Backup Verification:

- Schedule SQL Server Agent jobs to verify backups.
- Regularly review backup logs to confirm successful backups.

10. SQL Server Agent for Automating Backups

SQL Server Agent allows you to automate backups using scheduled jobs, ensuring consistent and timely backups without manual intervention.

Creating a Backup Job in SQL Server Agent:

1. In SSMS, go to **SQL Server Agent > Jobs > New Job**.
2. Name the job (e.g., DailyBackupJob).
3. Add **Steps** for each backup type (e.g., full, differential, log) with the appropriate SQL commands.
4. Set a **Schedule** for each step, such as weekly for full backups and daily for differential backups.
5. Enable **Notifications** to alert the database administrator if a backup job fails.

SQL Server Agent ensures that backups run on schedule and can alert you in case of issues.

11. Backing Up System Databases

SQL Server system databases—such as master, msdb, and model—contain essential configuration, job, and login information. Regular backups of these databases are essential for full recovery of the SQL Server environment.

Key System Databases to Back Up:

- **master**: Contains system-level information, including logins and configuration settings.
- **msdb**: Stores SQL Server Agent job information and backup history.
- **model**: Provides a template for new databases. Not critical but useful to back up after modifications.

Example of Backing Up System Databases:

sql

BACKUP DATABASE master TO DISK = 'D:\Backups\master.bak';
BACKUP DATABASE msdb TO DISK = 'D:\Backups\msdb.bak';
System database backups are typically scheduled weekly or whenever there are significant configuration changes.

12. Best Practices for Backup and Recovery

To ensure reliable backup and recovery in SQL Server, follow these best practices:

- **Choose the Right Recovery Model**: Match the recovery model to your data protection needs and acceptable data loss.
- **Use a Combination of Backups**: Regularly schedule full, differential, and transaction log backups to balance performance and recovery requirements.

- **Store Backups Securely**: Store backup files in a secure location and consider offsite storage for disaster recovery.

- **Verify and Test Backups Regularly**: Use RESTORE VERIFYONLY and periodically test restore operations to ensure backups are valid and restorable.

- **Automate Backups with SQL Server Agent**: Automate backups to ensure they run consistently, and enable alerts for failed backups.

- **Monitor Backup Storage and Rotation**: Regularly review and manage backup storage space and implement a retention policy to prevent unnecessary storage costs.

13. Disaster Recovery and Offsite Backups

For mission-critical databases, it's essential to implement a disaster recovery plan that includes offsite backups. Offsite backups provide additional protection in case of natural disasters or data center failures.

Offsite Backup Options:

- **Cloud Storage**: Store backups on cloud platforms like Azure or AWS for fast, secure access.
- **Physical Offsite Storage**: Transfer backup files to an offsite location using external storage devices.

- **Log Shipping**: Automates the backup and restore process between SQL Server instances for high availability and disaster recovery.

Example of Offsite Backup Strategy:

1. Schedule full backups to a local file path.
2. Use cloud backup software to replicate the local backup files to a secure cloud storage account.
3. Periodically test offsite backups for restoration to ensure disaster readiness.

An effective backup and recovery strategy is essential for protecting SQL Server data and ensuring business continuity in the face of unexpected events. This chapter covered SQL Server backup types, recovery models, and best practices for creating a robust backup plan. By implementing a combination of full, differential, and transaction log backups, and using SQL Server Agent for automation, you can ensure that your data is protected and can be quickly restored when needed. In the next chapter, we'll cover SQL Server high availability and disaster recovery options, including clustering and replication, to further enhance database resilience.

CHAPTER 16: DATA WAREHOUSING WITH SQL SERVER

Overview

A **data warehouse** is a centralized repository that aggregates and organizes data from multiple sources to support analysis and reporting. SQL Server offers several features to build, manage, and optimize data warehouses, making it an ideal platform for business intelligence (BI) solutions. In this chapter, we'll cover the essentials of data warehousing with SQL Server, including data modeling, Extract, Transform, Load (ETL) processes, indexing strategies, and best practices for optimizing a data warehouse for analytical workloads.

1. What is a Data Warehouse?

A data warehouse stores large volumes of historical data that can be queried and analyzed to support decision-making. Unlike transactional databases, which are optimized for fast reads and writes, data warehouses are optimized for complex queries, aggregations, and reporting.

Characteristics of a Data Warehouse:

- **Subject-Oriented**: Organizes data around specific business subjects, such as sales, finance, or customer activity.

- **Integrated**: Aggregates data from multiple sources in a consistent format.

- **Non-Volatile**: Data is not modified after it's loaded, allowing for historical analysis.

- **Time-Variant**: Stores data over time to support trend analysis and historical comparisons.

SQL Server provides tools like SQL Server Integration Services (SSIS), Analysis Services (SSAS), and PolyBase to facilitate data warehousing and BI tasks.

2. Data Warehouse Architecture

A typical data warehouse architecture includes:

1. **Data Sources**: Systems where data originates, such as transactional databases, ERP systems, CRM systems, and external data feeds.

2. **ETL Process**: Extract, Transform, and Load (ETL) moves data from sources into the data warehouse, transforming it to a consistent format.

3. **Data Storage Layer**: Central repository, often organized into fact and dimension tables.

4. **Data Access Layer**: Provides access to data for BI tools and reports.

SQL Server supports these layers with integration tools, high-performance storage, and query optimization for efficient data processing and reporting.

3. Data Modeling for Data Warehousing

Data modeling is essential for structuring a data warehouse to support efficient queries and reporting. The two most common data warehouse modeling techniques are **Star Schema** and **Snowflake Schema**.

Star Schema:

- **Fact Table**: Contains quantitative data for analysis, such as sales amount, quantity, and revenue.
- **Dimension Tables**: Contain descriptive attributes related to facts, such as date, product, or customer.

In a star schema, the fact table is at the center, with dimension tables around it, forming a star-like shape.

Example of a Star Schema:

- **FactSales** table: Stores sales metrics (e.g., SaleID, DateID, ProductID, CustomerID, Amount).
- **DimDate** table: Stores date information (e.g., DateID, Year, Month, Day).
- **DimProduct** table: Stores product details (e.g., ProductID, ProductName, Category).

Snowflake Schema: In a snowflake schema, dimensions are normalized into multiple related tables, reducing redundancy but increasing complexity.

4. Extract, Transform, Load (ETL) Process

The **ETL process** is responsible for moving data from source systems into the data warehouse. In SQL Server, SQL Server Integration Services (SSIS) is the primary tool for building ETL workflows.

ETL Stages:

1. **Extract**: Retrieve data from source systems, which may include multiple databases, flat files, or web services.
2. **Transform**: Cleanse, filter, and reformat data to ensure consistency and accuracy.
3. **Load**: Insert the transformed data into the data warehouse tables.

Using SSIS for ETL: SSIS provides a drag-and-drop interface for creating ETL packages, allowing you to define data flows, transformations, and error handling.

Example SSIS Transformations:

- **Data Conversion**: Converts data types to ensure compatibility with the data warehouse schema.

- **Lookup**: Enriches data by looking up related values from other tables.
- **Aggregation**: Pre-calculates metrics to speed up reporting.

5. Indexing Strategies for Data Warehouses

Indexes play a crucial role in optimizing query performance in data warehouses, where queries often involve aggregations, joins, and filtering on large datasets.

Types of Indexes for Data Warehousing:

- **Clustered Index**: Organizes data rows in the table based on the indexed columns. A clustered index on the primary key of fact tables improves data retrieval performance.
- **Non-Clustered Index**: Useful for frequently filtered columns in dimension tables, helping speed up queries that join on these columns.
- **Columnstore Index**: Stores data in a column-based format rather than row-based. Columnstore indexes are ideal for analytical workloads, as they provide high compression and faster access to large datasets.

Creating a Columnstore Index:

sql

```
CREATE    CLUSTERED    COLUMNSTORE    INDEX
idx_Columnstore ON FactSales;
```

Columnstore indexes improve performance for large fact tables and reduce storage requirements, making them essential for modern data warehousing.

6. Partitioning for Large Tables

Partitioning divides large tables into smaller, more manageable segments, which improves query performance and simplifies maintenance. SQL Server supports **table partitioning** to divide tables based on a specified column, typically a date.

Example of Partitioning a Sales Table by Date:

```sql
sql
CREATE PARTITION FUNCTION SalesDateRange (DATE)
AS RANGE RIGHT FOR VALUES ('2022-01-01', '2023-01-01');


CREATE PARTITION SCHEME SalesScheme
AS PARTITION SalesDateRange
TO (FileGroup1, FileGroup2, FileGroup3);


CREATE TABLE FactSales (
    SaleID INT,
    SaleDate DATE,
    Amount DECIMAL(10, 2)
)
ON SalesScheme (SaleDate);
```

This example partitions the FactSales table by SaleDate, storing data in different file groups based on the year. Partitioning improves query performance for large tables by restricting queries to specific partitions.

7. Data Aggregation for Performance Optimization

Data warehouses often store large volumes of data, and aggregating data at various levels can improve performance for reporting and analysis. **Aggregation tables** or **summary tables** pre-calculate metrics, allowing reports to retrieve data faster.

Example: Create a summary table for monthly sales totals.

```sql
CREATE TABLE MonthlySalesSummary AS
SELECT ProductID, YEAR(SaleDate) AS SaleYear,
MONTH(SaleDate) AS SaleMonth, SUM(Amount) AS TotalSales
FROM FactSales
GROUP BY ProductID, YEAR(SaleDate), MONTH(SaleDate);
```

Aggregating data at different levels (e.g., daily, monthly) allows for faster reporting and reduces the load on the main fact tables.

8. Slowly Changing Dimensions (SCD)

A **slowly changing dimension** (SCD) captures changes in dimension data over time. SQL Server supports different strategies for handling slowly changing dimensions, including **Type 1** and **Type 2**:

- **Type 1 SCD**: Overwrites old data with new data. Useful when historical accuracy isn't required.
- **Type 2 SCD**: Preserves history by adding new records for changes, allowing you to track changes over time.

Implementing Type 2 SCD:

sql

```
ALTER TABLE DimProduct ADD StartDate DATE, EndDate DATE;


-- Insert a new version of the product with updated details
INSERT INTO DimProduct (ProductID, ProductName, Category, StartDate, EndDate)
VALUES (1, 'Updated Product Name', 'Updated Category', GETDATE(), NULL);
```

Type 2 SCDs are commonly used in data warehouses to support historical analysis.

9. *SQL Server Analysis Services (SSAS)*

SQL Server Analysis Services (SSAS) is an OLAP (Online Analytical Processing) and data mining tool that allows you to build multidimensional and tabular models for advanced analytics. SSAS enhances the analytical capabilities of SQL Server by pre-aggregating data and providing fast query performance for BI applications.

Key Components of SSAS:

- **Cubes**: Multidimensional structures that organize data in measures (quantitative data) and dimensions (qualitative data).
- **Dimensions**: Categories by which data is sliced, such as time, product, or region.
- **Measures**: Numeric data points aggregated within dimensions, such as sales amount or quantity sold.

Creating an SSAS Cube:

1. In SQL Server Data Tools (SSDT), create an Analysis Services project.
2. Define data sources and data source views for accessing data warehouse tables.
3. Define dimensions and measures for the cube.
4. Process the cube to pre-aggregate data, enabling fast query responses.

SSAS provides optimized structures for interactive analysis, ideal for complex reporting requirements.

10. PolyBase for Big Data Integration

PolyBase allows SQL Server to integrate with external data sources, including Hadoop, Azure Blob Storage, and external SQL Server instances. PolyBase is useful for expanding data warehouses by incorporating big data sources without the need to migrate data.

Example of Querying External Data with PolyBase:

1. Configure PolyBase and set up an external data source.
2. Define external tables to access the data.

```sql
CREATE EXTERNAL TABLE ExternalSalesData (
    SaleID INT,
    SaleDate DATE,
    Amount DECIMAL(10,2)
)
WITH (
    LOCATION = 'sales_data/',
    DATA_SOURCE = ExternalDataSource,
    FILE_FORMAT = ExternalFileFormat
);
```

PolyBase allows you to query and join external data with local data, making it easier to build a comprehensive data warehouse that includes big data.

11. Data Warehouse Best Practices

Follow these best practices to build an efficient and scalable data warehouse in SQL Server:

- **Design for Query Performance**: Use star schemas and denormalized tables to optimize for read-heavy analytical workloads.

- **Partition Large Fact Tables**: Partition large tables by time or other relevant dimensions to improve performance.

- **Use Columnstore Indexes**: Leverage columnstore indexes on fact tables for high compression and fast query performance.

- **Implement ETL Error Handling**: Use SSIS error handling to capture and log errors during ETL processes.

- **Archive Old Data**: Move historical data to separate storage or archive tables to maintain performance.

- **Regularly Update Aggregations and Summary Tables**: Keep summary tables updated to ensure fast query responses for reporting.

12. Monitoring and Managing the Data Warehouse

Monitoring a data warehouse involves tracking query performance, storage usage, and ETL job success to ensure that the system operates efficiently.

Key Monitoring Tools:

- **SQL Server Management Studio (SSMS)**: Monitor query performance, storage, and index usage.

- **SQL Server Agent**: Automate ETL jobs, backups, and index maintenance.
- **Dynamic Management Views (DMVs)**: Analyze query performance and resource usage.

Example: Monitor the usage of columnstore indexes.

sql

Copy code

```sql
SELECT object_name(i.object_id) AS TableName, i.name AS IndexName, i.type_desc AS IndexType
FROM sys.indexes AS i
WHERE i.type_desc = 'CLUSTERED COLUMNSTORE';
```

This query lists all columnstore indexes, allowing you to ensure that indexes are in place for optimized performance

Data warehousing in SQL Server enables businesses to consolidate data from multiple sources, optimize it for analytical workloads, and support decision-making. This chapter covered the essentials of building a data warehouse, including data modeling, ETL processes with SSIS, indexing strategies, and tools like SSAS and PolyBase. By following best practices and leveraging SQL Server's powerful data warehousing features, you can create a high-performance data warehouse that serves as a foundation for business intelligence and analytics. In the next chapter, we'll explore SQL Server performance tuning techniques to further enhance the efficiency of your SQL Server environment

CHAPTER 17: SQL SERVER INTEGRATION SERVICES (SSIS)

Overview

SQL Server Integration Services (SSIS) is a powerful data integration and workflow application provided by SQL Server for performing Extract, Transform, and Load (ETL) operations. SSIS enables you to move and transform data from various sources into SQL Server databases, making it an essential tool for data warehousing, data migration, and business intelligence. In this chapter, we'll explore the core components of SSIS, walk through creating ETL packages, and discuss best practices for managing SSIS projects effectively.

1. Key Concepts in SSIS

SSIS consists of several components that enable the design, execution, and management of data flows and workflows:

- **Control Flow**: Manages the workflow and sequence of tasks in an SSIS package, allowing you to define the logic and flow of ETL operations.

- **Data Flow**: Responsible for extracting, transforming, and loading data. The data flow includes source, transformation, and destination components.
- **Connection Managers**: Define connections to data sources and destinations, such as SQL Server, flat files, and Excel files.
- **Variables**: Store values that can be used throughout the SSIS package, useful for parameterizing data flows and tasks.

2. SSIS Architecture and Package Structure

An **SSIS package** is a collection of tasks, data flows, variables, and configurations that define a data integration workflow. The primary components of a package include:

- **Tasks**: Each task performs a specific action, such as executing a SQL statement, sending an email, or transferring data between systems.
- **Precedence Constraints**: Define the flow between tasks, indicating when a task should run based on the success, failure, or completion of previous tasks.
- **Event Handlers**: Respond to package events (e.g., errors) by defining tasks that run automatically in response to these events.
- **Logging**: Allows for tracking package execution details, which is useful for troubleshooting and auditing.

SSIS packages can be created and managed using **SQL Server Data Tools (SSDT)**, a visual development environment.

3. Control Flow in SSIS

The **Control Flow** in SSIS defines the order and execution of tasks within a package. Control flow tasks are connected using **precedence constraints** to control when tasks should execute.

Common Control Flow Tasks:

- **Data Flow Task**: Moves data from sources to destinations, applying transformations along the way.
- **Execute SQL Task**: Runs SQL statements or stored procedures, useful for pre-processing or post-processing steps.
- **File System Task**: Performs file system operations, such as moving, deleting, or copying files.
- **Script Task**: Allows for custom code using C# or VB.NET, useful for advanced logic not covered by standard tasks.
- **Send Mail Task**: Sends email notifications, often used for alerting on package completion or errors.

Example Control Flow: Create a package that moves a file to an archive folder after loading it into a database.

1. **Data Flow Task**: Load data from a flat file into a SQL Server table.

2. **File System Task**: Move the file to an archive folder after loading.

3. **Send Mail Task**: Notify an administrator of the package's success or failure.

4. Data Flow in SSIS

The **Data Flow** is where data is extracted, transformed, and loaded, making it a core component of SSIS for ETL processes. A data flow contains three types of components:

1. **Sources**: Define the origin of the data, such as SQL Server, flat files, Excel files, or other databases.

2. **Transformations**: Modify, cleanse, or reshape the data. Transformations can include sorting, aggregating, or performing lookups.

3. **Destinations**: Define where the transformed data will be loaded, typically into SQL Server tables, files, or other destinations.

Example Data Flow Components:

- **OLE DB Source**: Extracts data from an SQL Server database.

- **Lookup Transformation**: Matches source data with reference data to enrich the data flow.

- **Derived Column Transformation**: Creates new columns or modifies existing columns.
- **Conditional Split Transformation**: Routes data to different paths based on conditions.
- **OLE DB Destination**: Loads data into a SQL Server table.

5. Building an ETL Process in SSIS

An ETL process in SSIS generally includes the following steps:

1. **Extract**: Use data sources to retrieve data from multiple systems, such as databases, files, or external applications.
2. **Transform**: Apply transformations to clean, format, and modify the data for consistency.
3. **Load**: Load the transformed data into the data warehouse or destination database.

Example of an ETL Process in SSIS:

1. **Control Flow**: Define the order of tasks, including loading data, archiving files, and sending notifications.
2. **Data Flow**: Extract data from multiple tables, apply transformations to clean and standardize the data, and load it into the destination database.

6. Transformations in SSIS

Transformations are applied within the data flow to cleanse and format data before it reaches the destination. Some key transformations include:

- **Aggregate**: Summarizes data, useful for grouping and calculating totals.
- **Conditional Split**: Directs data rows to different outputs based on a condition, allowing for different processing paths.
- **Derived Column**: Creates new columns based on expressions, such as calculating new values or concatenating strings.
- **Lookup**: Joins incoming data with a reference table to enrich the dataset.
- **Sort**: Sorts data by specified columns, often required for merging or deduplication.
- **Data Conversion**: Converts columns to different data types to ensure compatibility with destination tables.

Example: Use the Conditional Split transformation to separate high-value and low-value orders for different processing paths.

7. Connection Managers

Connection Managers in SSIS define the connections to data sources and destinations, such as databases, flat files, and web services. SSIS includes built-in connection managers for common sources, including SQL Server, Excel, OLE DB, and ADO.NET.

Creating a Connection Manager:

1. Right-click on **Connection Managers** in SSIS and choose **New Connection**.
2. Select the connection type (e.g., OLE DB, Flat File).
3. Configure the connection by providing necessary details, such as server name, database, file path, and credentials.

Using parameters and expressions within connection managers allows for flexibility, enabling connection settings to be updated at runtime.

8. Error Handling and Logging in SSIS

SSIS provides several mechanisms for handling errors and logging package execution, which are critical for troubleshooting and ensuring data quality.

Error Handling:

- **Error Output**: Many data flow components allow you to direct rows that encounter errors to a separate output, enabling you to log or handle them differently.
- **Event Handlers**: Define tasks to respond to specific events, such as OnError or OnWarning, allowing you to respond to errors with notifications, logging, or custom actions.

Example of Error Handling with Error Output: In a Data Flow Task, configure the destination component's error output to redirect rows with errors to an error log table for further analysis.

Logging: SSIS supports logging to capture package execution details. You can log to multiple targets, including SQL Server, text files, and Windows Event Logs.

Enabling Logging:

1. Right-click on the package in SSDT and select **Logging**.
2. Choose the log provider (e.g., SQL Server, text file).
3. Select events to log, such as OnError, OnWarning, and OnInformation.

9. Deploying SSIS Packages

Once an SSIS package is developed and tested, it can be deployed to SQL Server for production use. SQL Server provides several options for deployment:

- **SQL Server Deployment**: Deploy the package to the SSISDB catalog on SQL Server, making it centrally accessible and manageable.
- **File System Deployment**: Deploy the package to a folder on the server, useful for environments without SSISDB.
- **Integration Services Catalogs (SSISDB)**: The SSISDB catalog provides a managed environment for deploying,

configuring, and executing SSIS packages, with support for logging, versioning, and troubleshooting.

Deploying to SSISDB:

1. Right-click on the SSIS project in SSDT and select **Deploy**.
2. Choose **SSIS in SQL Server** and specify the server and path in the SSISDB catalog.
3. Follow the wizard to complete the deployment.

10. Autmating SSIS Packages with SQL Server Agent

SQL Server Agent allows you to schedule SSIS packages, automating ETL processes to run at specific times or intervals.

Scheduling an SSIS Package:

1. In SQL Server Management Studio (SSMS), open **SQL Server Agent** and create a new job.
2. Add a **New Step**, set the **Type** to **SQL Server Integration Services Package**, and select the package from SSISDB.
3. Define the **Schedule** for the job, such as daily, weekly, or based on specific intervals.

SQL Server Agent will execute the SSIS package automatically, enabling regular data integration without manual intervention.

11. SSIS Best Practices

Following best practices ensures that your SSIS packages are efficient, maintainable, and reliable:

- **Design Modular Packages**: Break down large ETL processes into smaller, modular packages that can be reused and managed independently.
- **Use Logging and Error Handling**: Enable logging and configure error handling to troubleshoot issues effectively.
- **Optimize Data Flow**: Use transformations only when necessary, and avoid using row-by-row processing where possible.
- **Parameterize Connection Strings**: Use parameters or variables to configure connection strings dynamically, allowing for easier deployment across environments.
- **Minimize Memory Usage**: Configure data flow buffers to prevent memory overload in large data flows.
- **Test with Production-Like Data**: Test SSIS packages with realistic data volumes to identify and resolve performance bottlenecks.

12. Monitoring and Troubleshooting SSIS Packages

Monitoring and troubleshooting SSIS packages are essential for ensuring data accuracy and performance.

Using SSISDB Catalog Views: The SSISDB catalog provides several catalog views for monitoring and troubleshooting package executions, including catalog.executions and catalog.event_messages.

Example: Query SSIS package execution history.

sql

Copy code

```sql
SELECT e.execution_id, e.start_time, e.end_time, e.status, m.message
FROM catalog.executions AS e
JOIN catalog.event_messages AS m ON e.execution_id = m.execution_id
WHERE e.package_name = 'MyETLPackage'
ORDER BY e.start_time DESC;
```

This query retrieves the execution history for a specific SSIS package, helping you identify errors or performance issues.

SQL Server Integration Services (SSIS) is a powerful tool for ETL operations, data migration, and automation, making it a central component in data warehousing and business intelligence solutions. This chapter covered SSIS components, data flow design, control flow, error handling, and best practices for deploying and managing packages. By using SSIS effectively, you can build robust data integration workflows that ensure accurate and timely data delivery for analytics and reporting. In the next chapter, we'll delve into SQL Server Analysis Services (SSAS) for advanced analytical processing and multidimensional data modeling

CHAPTER 18: SQL SERVER REPORTING SERVICES (SSRS)

Overview

SQL Server Reporting Services (SSRS) is a server-based report generating software that allows you to design, manage, and deliver reports in a variety of formats. SSRS enables organizations to create complex reports from relational and multidimensional data sources, helping users gain insights and make data-driven decisions. In this chapter, we'll explore SSRS's core components, how to design and deploy reports, and best practices for managing reports in SQL Server.

1. Key Concepts in SSRS

SSRS provides a range of tools for creating, managing, and delivering reports:

- **Report Designer**: A tool within SQL Server Data Tools (SSDT) or Microsoft Visual Studio for designing reports. Report Designer provides a graphical interface for building reports.
- **Report Builder**: A standalone application for building and editing reports, typically used by business users for ad hoc reporting.

- **Report Server**: The server environment where reports are hosted, managed, and delivered to users. The report server handles report processing, rendering, and access control.
- **Report Manager**: A web-based interface for managing and viewing reports. Administrators and users can access, organize, and run reports here.

2. SSRS Architecture and Report Components

SSRS follows a client-server architecture, with reports stored and processed on the **Report Server** and accessed by users through web-based or application-based interfaces.

Core Components of an SSRS Report:

- **Data Sources**: Connections to databases, files, or other sources from which report data is pulled.
- **Datasets**: Queries or stored procedures that retrieve data for the report.
- **Report Items**: Elements in a report, such as tables, charts, matrices, and images.
- **Expressions**: Custom calculations or logic applied within reports, written in an expression language similar to Visual Basic.

3. Creating a Basic Report in SSRS

To create a report in SSRS, you typically use **SQL Server Data Tools (SSDT)** or **Report Builder**:

1. **Define Data Sources**: Establish connections to data sources, such as SQL Server databases.
2. **Create Datasets**: Write queries or stored procedures to retrieve data for the report.
3. **Design the Layout**: Add tables, charts, and text boxes to display data and create a cohesive report.
4. **Preview and Test**: Run the report to verify data accuracy and design layout.
5. **Deploy the Report**: Publish the report to the report server for user access.

Example: Create a simple report showing total sales by product category.

1. Define a data source connecting to the sales database.
2. Create a dataset with a query that aggregates sales by category.
3. Add a table to display the results, grouping data by product category.
4. Format the table with headers, borders, and appropriate number formatting.
5. Preview the report to verify the layout and accuracy.

4. Working with Data Sources and Datasets

SSRS reports require **data sources** and **datasets** to retrieve data. Data sources define the connection to a database, while datasets represent the data retrieved by a specific query.

Creating a Shared Data Source:

1. In Report Designer, right-click **Data Sources** and select **Add Data Source**.
2. Choose **Use a shared connection or report model** or **Embedded connection**.
3. Configure the connection string and authentication method.

Creating a Dataset:

1. Right-click on **Datasets** in Report Designer and select **Add Dataset**.
2. Choose to use an existing data source and enter the SQL query or select a stored procedure.
3. Define parameters if needed and preview the dataset to confirm data retrieval.

Example Dataset:

```sql
Copy code
SELECT CategoryName, SUM(SalesAmount) AS TotalSales
FROM Sales
```

GROUP BY CategoryName;

This dataset retrieves total sales for each product category, which can be displayed in a table or chart in the report.

5. Designing Report Layouts

SSRS offers a variety of tools to customize report layouts, including tables, matrices, lists, and charts. Each element allows for different data presentations and formatting options.

Common Report Items:

- **Table**: Used to display data in a tabular format. Ideal for listing records with multiple columns.
- **Matrix**: Similar to a pivot table, allowing data to be grouped by rows and columns dynamically.
- **List**: A flexible container for free-form layout, useful for creating custom report layouts.
- **Chart**: Used for visualizing data with charts, including bar, line, pie, and area charts.

Example: Design a report with a table and a chart.

1. Insert a table to display detailed sales data by product, SELECT ProductName, SalesAmount

FROM Sales
WHERE Category = @Category;

In this example, the @Category parameter allows users to filter the report by a specific product category at runtime.

---

7. Expressions and Calculated Fields

Expressions in SSRS are used to create dynamic content, format values, or apply conditional logic. Expressions are written in an expression language similar to Visual Basic and can be used throughout the report.

Common Uses of Expressions:

- **Calculated Fields**: Create custom calculations, such as =Fields!Quantity.Value * Fields!Price.Value.
- **Conditional Formatting**: Apply formatting based on data values, such as changing text color for negative values.
- **Dynamic Text**: Display values based on parameters or dataset values.

Example of Conditional Formatting:

vb
=IIF(Fields!SalesAmount.Value < 0, "Red", "Black")
This expression changes the text color to red if SalesAmount is negative, useful for highlighting losses in a financial report.

8. Creating Charts and Visualizations

SSRS supports a variety of chart types to visualize data, making reports more insightful and easier to interpret.

Common Chart Types:

- **Bar Chart**: Ideal for comparing values across categories.
- **Line Chart**: Useful for showing trends over time.
- **Pie Chart**: Represents proportions of a whole, suitable for showing percentages.
- **Area Chart**: Similar to line charts but fills the area below the line, emphasizing the magnitude of values.

Example of Creating a Line Chart:

1. Add a line chart to the report design area.
2. Set the **Category** axis to display months and the **Value** axis to show total sales.
3. Customize the chart with labels, gridlines, and colors for better readability.

9. Deploying and Publishing Reports

Once a report is complete, it can be deployed to the **Report Server** to make it available to users.

Steps to Deploy a Report:

1. Configure the target server in **Project Properties** under **TargetServerURL**.

2. Right-click on the project in SSDT and select **Deploy**.

3. Access the report on the Report Server through the **Report Manager** or **Web Portal**.

Deployed reports can be organized into folders and secured by setting permissions for different user groups, controlling access to specific reports.

10. Managing and Securing Reports

SSRS provides a variety of tools for managing and securing reports to ensure data is accessible only to authorized users.

Security and Permissions:

- **Role-Based Security**: SSRS uses roles such as **Browser**, **Publisher**, and **Report Builder** to control access to reports and folders.
- **Item-Level Security**: Define permissions on individual reports or folders, allowing different access levels for different users or groups.

Example: Grant a user read-only access to a folder of financial reports.

1. In the Report Manager, navigate to the folder and open **Folder Settings**.

2. Add the user or group and assign them the **Browser** role, granting them view-only permissions.

11. Scheduling and Subscribing to Reports

SSRS allows users to schedule and subscribe to reports, enabling automated delivery at specified times.

Report Subscriptions:

1. Users can subscribe to reports through the **Report Manager** by specifying delivery options such as email or file share.
2. Define a schedule (e.g., daily, weekly) for automatic report generation and delivery.
3. Configure report parameters for subscriptions to customize the data each user receives.

Example of a Subscription: A finance team subscribes to a weekly sales report that is emailed every Monday morning, allowing them to review the previous week's sales trends.

12. SSRS Best Practices

Following best practices helps ensure SSRS reports are efficient, maintainable, and user-friendly:

- **Optimize Queries**: Write efficient queries to reduce report processing time, especially for large datasets.

- **Use Shared Data Sources**: Use shared data sources to streamline management and reduce redundancy.

- **Design for Performance**: Limit the number of complex calculations in the report and use pre-aggregated data if possible.

- **Implement Consistent Formatting**: Use consistent fonts, colors, and styles for a professional look and better readability.

- **Test with Different Parameters**: Verify that reports display correctly with various parameter values, especially if parameters affect layout or data.

13. Monitoring and Troubleshooting SSRS

SSRS includes tools for monitoring report usage and troubleshooting issues:

- **Execution Log**: SSRS maintains an execution log that captures details about report processing, including performance metrics and errors.

- **Performance Monitoring**: Use SQL Server's Performance Monitor counters to track SSRS resource usage.

- **Error Logs**: Review SSRS error logs for information about failed report executions or deployment issues.

Example: Query the SSRS execution log to analyze report performance.

sql

```
SELECT TimeStart, TimeEnd, ReportPath, Status
FROM ReportServer.dbo.ExecutionLog3
WHERE ReportPath = '/SalesReports/MonthlySales'
ORDER BY TimeStart DESC;
```

This query retrieves execution details for a specific report, helping you identify performance issues or errors.

SQL Server Reporting Services (SSRS) provides a comprehensive suite of tools for designing, deploying, and managing reports, making it an invaluable resource for business intelligence and data-driven decision-making. This chapter covered the core components of SSRS, including report design, data sources, parameters, deployment, and subscriptions, as well as best practices for creating effective reports. By leveraging SSRS, you can transform data into insightful reports that support your organization's strategic goals. In the next chapter, we'll explore SQL Server Analysis Services (SSAS) for multidimensional and tabular data modeling, adding further analytical capabilities to your SQL Server environment.

CHAPTER 19: SQL SERVER ANALYSIS SERVICES (SSAS)

Overview

SQL Server Analysis Services (SSAS) is a data analysis and reporting technology that enables you to build multidimensional (OLAP) and tabular models to support advanced analytics and business intelligence. SSAS is designed for complex analytical processing, allowing users to quickly explore and analyze large datasets. In this chapter, we'll explore the basics of SSAS, its different models, how to create cubes and tabular models, and best practices for optimizing analytical solutions with SSAS.

1. Understanding SSAS Models

SSAS supports two primary modeling approaches: **Multidimensional (OLAP)** and **Tabular**. Each model has its unique strengths, so the choice of model depends on your data complexity, reporting requirements, and user preferences.

- **Multidimensional Model (OLAP)**: Organizes data into multidimensional structures called cubes, with dimensions (e.g., Product, Time, Geography) and measures (e.g., Sales, Quantity). This model is ideal for handling complex calculations and hierarchies.

- **Tabular Model**: Organizes data into in-memory tables that resemble relational tables but optimized for analytical performance. Tabular models use a simplified structure, supporting faster deployment and ease of use, especially with Power BI and Excel.

Both models support data aggregation, calculations, and fast querying, but the Tabular model is often preferred for newer solutions due to its performance and flexibility.

2. SSAS Architecture

The core components of SSAS include:

- **Data Sources**: Define the connection to databases or other sources from which SSAS pulls data.
- **Data Source Views**: Logical views of the underlying data sources, which allow you to define relationships and filter data for use in SSAS.
- **Dimensions**: Define the descriptive data (e.g., Customer, Product) used to slice and dice measures.
- **Measures and Measure Groups**: Numeric data points that can be aggregated, such as Sales Amount or Quantity Sold.
- **Calculations**: Custom calculations, aggregations, and KPIs (Key Performance Indicators) used to enhance analytical reporting.

SSAS integrates with SQL Server Management Studio (SSMS) for management and SQL Server Data Tools (SSDT) for model design.

3. Creating a Multidimensional (OLAP) Cube in SSAS

A **cube** is a multidimensional data structure that allows users to analyze data from multiple perspectives. Cubes organize data into dimensions and measures, enabling fast access to aggregated data.

Steps to Create a Cube:

1. **Define the Data Source**: Create a data source to connect to the database.
2. **Create a Data Source View**: Define the tables and relationships from the data source that will be used in the cube.
3. **Define Dimensions**: Create dimensions based on the descriptive data, such as Time, Product, or Geography.
4. **Define Measures**: Create measure groups based on quantitative data, such as sales or order quantities.
5. **Build the Cube**: Add dimensions and measures to the cube, and configure aggregations.
6. **Deploy and Process the Cube**: Deploy the cube to the SSAS server and process it to load data.

Example: Create a Sales cube with the following structure:

- **Dimensions**: Product, Date, Customer

- **Measures**: Sales Amount, Quantity Sold

By organizing data this way, users can analyze sales by product, date, and customer, viewing metrics from multiple perspectives.

4. Designing Dimensions and Hierarchies

Dimensions are the descriptive attributes in a cube, providing context for measures. Each dimension can include **attributes** (individual columns, such as Product Name) and **hierarchies** (such as Year > Quarter > Month).

Creating a Dimension:

1. In SSDT, right-click on Dimensions and select **New Dimension**.
2. Select the table and columns you want to include in the dimension.
3. Define **hierarchies** by arranging related attributes in a sequence.

Example of a Date Hierarchy:

1. Create a Date dimension with attributes like Year, Quarter, and Month.
2. Arrange these attributes in a hierarchy (Year > Quarter > Month).

3. This hierarchy allows users to drill down from Year to Month in their analyses.

Hierarchies improve navigation within dimensions, allowing users to analyze data at different levels of granularity.

5. Defining Measures and Measure Groups

Measures are numeric data points, like sales revenue or quantity sold, which can be aggregated. **Measure Groups** are collections of related measures within a cube, often based on a single fact table.

Creating Measures:

1. In SSDT, select the cube, then click on **New Measure**.
2. Choose the column to be used for the measure, such as Sales Amount.
3. Configure the aggregation type (e.g., SUM, COUNT, AVERAGE) for each measure.

Example of Measures in a Sales Cube:

- **Total Sales**: SUM of Sales Amount
- **Total Quantity Sold**: SUM of Quantity
- **Average Sales**: AVERAGE of Sales Amount

Measure groups help organize measures logically, especially when you have measures from multiple fact tables.

6. Calculations and KPIs

SSAS allows you to create custom calculations and KPIs to enhance your analytical models. **MDX (Multidimensional Expressions)** is used in the Multidimensional model, while **DAX (Data Analysis Expressions)** is used in the Tabular model.

MDX Calculated Members: In the cube, you can define calculations such as profit margins, growth rates, or any other custom metric.

Example of a Calculated Measure (MDX):

mdx
Copy code
```
CREATE     MEMBER     CURRENTCUBE.[Measures].[Profit
Margin] AS
  [Measures].[Total Sales] - [Measures].[Total Cost]
```
KPIs: SSAS KPIs (Key Performance Indicators) are metrics with targets, often visualized with icons to show performance status (e.g., red, yellow, green).

Example of a KPI:

- **Measure**: Sales Amount
- **Goal**: Sales Target
- **Status**: Indicator showing performance against target

KPIs help users assess performance quickly and support decision-making by highlighting key metrics.

7. Creating a Tabular Model in SSAS

The **Tabular Model** in SSAS uses tables and columns and is optimized for in-memory performance. It supports both DAX calculations and relational concepts, making it easier to use for newer BI solutions.

Steps to Create a Tabular Model:

1. **Define the Data Source**: Create connections to the source data.
2. **Import Data**: Load data from tables or views into the model.
3. **Define Relationships**: Establish relationships between tables.
4. **Create Calculated Columns and Measures**: Use DAX to define custom calculations.
5. **Deploy and Process the Model**: Publish the model to SSAS for analysis.

Example: Create a Tabular model for a sales dashboard with tables for Products, Customers, and Orders.

- **Relationships**: Link Orders to Products by ProductID and Orders to Customers by CustomerID.

- **DAX Measures**: Define measures like Total Sales and Average Order Value using DAX.

Tabular models provide flexibility, especially when used with Power BI or Excel for self-service BI.

8. DAX Basics for Tabular Models

DAX (Data Analysis Expressions) is a formula language for defining custom calculations in Tabular models, Power BI, and Excel. DAX functions allow you to create measures, calculated columns, and tables.

Common DAX Functions:

- **SUM**: Aggregates a column of numbers.
- **AVERAGE**: Calculates the average value.
- **CALCULATE**: Modifies a measure's filter context.
- **IF**: Conditional logic.

Example of a DAX Measure:

dax

Copy code

Total Sales = SUM(Sales[SalesAmount])

Example of a DAX Calculation with Filters:

dax

Copy code

Sales Last Year = CALCULATE(SUM(Sales[SalesAmount]), DATEADD(Date[Date], -1, YEAR))

DAX is a powerful tool for creating dynamic and complex calculations in Tabular models, enhancing analytical capabilities.

9. Processing and Deploying SSAS Models

After designing an SSAS model, you must **process** it to load data into the model and calculate aggregations. SSAS provides several processing options, including **full processing** (reloads all data) and **incremental processing** (loads only new data).

Deploying an SSAS Model:

1. In SSDT, configure the server and database where the model will be deployed.
2. Right-click the project and select **Deploy**.
3. After deployment, process the model to make it accessible for querying.

Processing Options:

- **Full Process**: Reloads all data, ideal for initial deployment.
- **Process Add**: Loads only new or updated data, useful for scheduled updates.
- **Process Recalc**: Recalculates measures and KPIs without reloading data.

Regular processing ensures that the SSAS model has the latest data for accurate analysis.

10. Querying SSAS Models with MDX and DAX

MDX (Multidimensional Expressions) is used to query multidimensional (OLAP) models, while **DAX** is used for querying tabular models.

Example of an MDX Query:

mdx

Copy code

```
SELECT
  {[Measures].[Total Sales]} ON COLUMNS,
  {[Product].[Category].Members} ON ROWS
FROM [SalesCube]
```

This query retrieves Total Sales by Product Category from a multidimensional cube.

Example of a DAX Query:

dax

Copy code

```
EVALUATE
SUMMARIZE(
  Sales,
  Product[Category],
  "Total Sales", SUM(Sales[SalesAmount])
```

)

This DAX query summarizes Total Sales by Product Category, ideal for analysis in tabular models.

11. SSAS Best Practices

Follow best practices for designing efficient and scalable SSAS models:

- **Optimize Relationships and Indexes**: Create relationships between tables and define primary keys to improve query performance.
- **Use Hierarchies in Dimensions**: Define hierarchies in dimensions for easier navigation and efficient aggregations.
- **Limit Processing Time**: Schedule incremental processing when possible to reduce processing time.
- **Avoid Complex Calculations in Real-Time**: Pre-calculate values wherever possible to reduce runtime complexity.
- **Use Aggregations**: Define aggregations for commonly queried measures to improve performance.
- **Monitor Model Performance**: Use SSAS Profiler and SQL Server Performance Monitor to analyze and optimize SSAS processing.

12. Monitoring and Managing SSAS

SQL Server Management Studio (SSMS) provides tools to monitor and manage SSAS models. You can track processing time, query performance, and resource usage to optimize the model.

Monitoring Tools:

- **SSAS Profiler**: Captures events, including query execution and processing, helping you identify performance bottlenecks.
- **Dynamic Management Views (DMVs)**: Provide real-time insights into SSAS metadata, user activity, and memory usage.

Example DMV Query:

sql
Copy code

```
SELECT * FROM $System.DISCOVER_SESSIONS
```

This query retrieves information on active user sessions, helping you track model usage and performance.

SQL Server Analysis Services (SSAS) enables complex data modeling, fast querying, and interactive analysis for business intelligence. This chapter covered the essentials of creating multidimensional and tabular models, defining dimensions and measures, using MDX and DAX for custom calculations, and deploying models. With SSAS, you can build scalable analytical solutions that provide users with insights and support data-driven decision-making. In the next chapter, we'll explore performance tuning techniques to enhance SQL Server's efficiency across different use cases.

CHAPTER 20: MONITORING AND PERFORMANCE TUNING IN SQL SERVER

Overview

Monitoring and performance tuning are essential tasks for maintaining an efficient and reliable SQL Server environment. Proactive monitoring helps identify performance bottlenecks, while tuning techniques optimize queries, indexes, and configurations to improve response times and resource utilization. In this chapter, we'll explore SQL Server's monitoring tools, common performance issues, and best practices for tuning databases, queries, and indexes to achieve optimal performance.

1. Monitoring SQL Server with Built-in Tools

SQL Server provides several built-in tools for monitoring database performance, including:

- **SQL Server Management Studio (SSMS)**: The default interface for managing SQL Server, including tools for monitoring activity and viewing execution plans.
- **SQL Server Profiler**: Captures a trace of SQL Server events, helping identify slow-running queries, deadlocks, and resource-intensive operations.

- **Performance Monitor (PerfMon)**: A Windows tool that tracks system metrics like CPU, memory, disk I/O, and SQL Server-specific counters.
- **Extended Events**: Lightweight event-handling system that captures detailed information about server events, useful for advanced troubleshooting.
- **Dynamic Management Views (DMVs)**: Provide real-time insights into query execution, index usage, and resource consumption.

2. Using SQL Server Profiler and Extended Events

SQL Server Profiler allows you to capture and analyze a stream of events for specific activities on SQL Server. It is useful for troubleshooting slow queries, monitoring user activity, and identifying resource bottlenecks.

Using SQL Server Profiler:

1. Open **SQL Server Profiler** in SSMS and start a new trace.
2. Select a template, such as **Tuning** or **Standard**, based on your needs.
3. Define events to monitor, such as **RPC**

   for stored procedures or **SQL**

   for T-SQL statements.

4. Start the trace and analyze the captured data for performance issues.

Extended Events are more lightweight and efficient than SQL Server Profiler and are the recommended option for monitoring in production environments.

Creating an Extended Event Session:

1. In SSMS, expand **Management > Extended Events** and right-click **Sessions**, then select **New Session**.
2. Define the events to capture, such as sqlserver.sql_batch_completed.
3. Configure filters, data storage, and start the session.
4. Review the collected data to analyze SQL Server activity.

3. *Dynamic Management Views (DMVs) for Real-Time Monitoring*

Dynamic Management Views (DMVs) provide real-time information on SQL Server's performance, sessions, query execution, and indexes.

Common DMVs for Monitoring:

- **sys.dm_exec_requests**: Shows active requests and resource usage, including wait types and CPU time.

- **sys.dm_exec_query_stats**: Provides performance statistics for cached queries, helping identify slow-running queries.

- **sys.dm_db_index_usage_stats**: Tracks index usage, helping you identify unused or overused indexes.

- **sys.dm_os_wait_stats**: Shows wait types and times, which can help identify resource contention (e.g., locking, I/O waits).

Example DMV Query: Identify the top 10 longest-running queries.

sql

Copy code

```sql
SELECT TOP 10
    qs.total_elapsed_time / 1000 AS ElapsedTimeMs,
    qs.execution_count,
    q.text AS QueryText
FROM
    sys.dm_exec_query_stats AS qs
CROSS APPLY
    sys.dm_exec_sql_text(qs.sql_handle) AS q
ORDER BY
    ElapsedTimeMs DESC;
```

This query retrieves the longest-running queries based on elapsed time, helping you identify queries to optimize.

4. SQL Server Wait Statistics

Wait statistics provide insights into the types of waits that occur when SQL Server queries wait for resources. By analyzing wait types, you can diagnose common performance issues.

Common Wait Types:

- **CXPACKET**: Indicates parallelism waits, often caused by inefficient query plans.
- **PAGEIOLATCH**: Indicates I/O waits, commonly caused by disk bottlenecks.
- **LCK_M**: Indicates locking waits, caused by concurrency issues.
- **SOS_SCHEDULER_YIELD**: Indicates CPU waits, often due to CPU-intensive queries.

Example of Viewing Wait Statistics:

sql
Copy code

```sql
SELECT wait_type, SUM(wait_time_ms) AS WaitTimeMs
FROM sys.dm_os_wait_stats
GROUP BY wait_type
ORDER BY WaitTimeMs DESC;
```

This query shows wait types ordered by total wait time, helping you identify major performance bottlenecks.

5. Query Performance Tuning

Query tuning is essential for optimizing SQL Server's performance. Common query optimization techniques include:

1. **Review Execution Plans**: Examine execution plans to understand how SQL Server retrieves data. Look for operations like table scans and nested loops that can cause slowdowns.

2. **Optimize Joins**: Use appropriate join types and ensure indexes are available on join columns.

3. **Use Indexes Efficiently**: Ensure that filters in WHERE and JOIN clauses use indexed columns.

4. **Minimize Use of Cursors**: Avoid cursors when possible, as they perform row-by-row processing. Use set-based operations instead.

5. **Avoid Scalar Functions in Queries**: Scalar functions in SELECT or WHERE clauses can slow down queries. Use computed columns or table-valued functions where possible.

6. **Use Stored Procedures**: Stored procedures are precompiled, which can improve performance for frequently executed queries.

Example: Reviewing an Execution Plan in SSMS

1. Run the query and enable the **Display Actual Execution Plan** option in SSMS.

2. Look for warning signs, such as **Table Scan** (indicating no index) or **Nested Loops** on large tables.
3. Apply index optimizations or rewrite the query as needed.

6. Index Optimization and Maintenance

Indexes are essential for query performance, but they require regular maintenance to stay efficient. Proper indexing and index maintenance can drastically improve query response times.

Indexing Best Practices:

- **Create Indexes on Frequently Queried Columns**: Use indexes on columns that appear in WHERE, JOIN, or ORDER BY clauses.
- **Use Composite Indexes for Multi-Column Queries**: Composite indexes optimize queries that filter on multiple columns.
- **Limit the Number of Indexes on Write-Heavy Tables**: Indexes slow down INSERT, UPDATE, and DELETE operations, so use them judiciously on frequently modified tables.

Index Maintenance:

- **Rebuild Indexes**: Rebuild fragmented indexes to improve query performance. Use ALTER INDEX ... REBUILD.

- **Reorganize Indexes**: Reorganize less fragmented indexes for a lighter maintenance operation. Use ALTER INDEX ... REORGANIZE.

- **Update Statistics**: SQL Server uses statistics to create efficient query plans. Update statistics regularly with UPDATE STATISTICS or use AUTO UPDATE STATISTICS.

Example of Rebuilding an Index:

sql

ALTER INDEX idx_EmployeeName ON Employees REBUILD;

This command rebuilds the idx_EmployeeName index, reducing fragmentation and improving performance.

7. Configuring SQL Server Memory and CPU Settings

SQL Server automatically allocates resources, but you can fine-tune these settings based on workload requirements.

Memory Configuration:

- **Max Server Memory**: Limit the maximum memory available to SQL Server to prevent it from using all system memory.

  sql
  Copy code

EXEC sp_configure 'max server memory', 8192; -- sets max memory to 8GB
RECONFIGURE;

- **Min Server Memory**: Set a minimum memory threshold to ensure SQL Server retains enough memory for consistent performance.

CPU Configuration:

- **Max Degree of Parallelism (MAXDOP)**: Controls the number of CPUs used for parallel query execution. For OLTP workloads, setting MAXDOP to 1 may help reduce contention.

sql
EXEC sp_configure 'max degree of parallelism', 4; -- limits parallelism to 4 CPUs
RECONFIGURE;

Example: Setting max server memory to prevent SQL Server from over-consuming memory and affecting other applications.

8. Disk I/O and TempDB Optimization

Disk I/O and TempDB configuration play a crucial role in SQL Server performance. Ensuring sufficient I/O capacity and optimizing TempDB can prevent bottlenecks.

TempDB Best Practices:

- **Separate TempDB onto Dedicated Disks**: Place TempDB on high-performance storage to reduce contention.
- **Increase TempDB Files**: Set TempDB to use multiple files (one per CPU core up to 8) to balance I/O.

sql

Copy code

```
ALTER DATABASE TempDB ADD FILE (NAME = N'Tempdev2', FILENAME = N'<path>\Tempdev2.ndf', SIZE = 512MB);
```

- **Configure TempDB Growth**: Set TempDB files to grow in fixed increments (e.g., 512MB) to avoid performance issues from auto-growth.

9. Monitoring and Managing Locks and Deadlocks

Locks and deadlocks can impact performance by causing contention between transactions. Monitoring locking behavior helps identify and resolve blocking issues.

Identifying Locks:

- Use sys.dm_tran_locks to view active locks and their types.

sql

Copy code

SELECT * FROM sys.dm_tran_locks;

Detecting Deadlocks:

- Enable the **Deadlock Graph** event in Extended Events to capture deadlock details.
- Use SET DEADLOCK_PRIORITY LOW in non-critical transactions to minimize deadlock impact.

Resolving Deadlocks:

- **Reduce Locking Scope**: Avoid locking rows unless necessary. Use READ COMMITTED isolation level.
- **Optimize Transaction Length**: Keep transactions short to reduce lock wait times.
- **Add Appropriate Indexes**: Ensure that queries on frequently accessed tables are properly indexed to reduce locking time.

10. SQL Server Performance Tuning Best Practices

Follow these best practices to maintain a high-performance SQL Server environment:

- **Index Regularly**: Ensure indexes are created on frequently queried columns and maintained regularly.

- **Optimize Queries**: Review query execution plans and rewrite poorly performing queries.

- **Configure Memory and CPU Settings**: Set memory limits and configure CPU settings based on workload requirements.

- **Monitor TempDB Usage**: Place TempDB on fast storage, add multiple files, and monitor for contention.

- **Review Wait Statistics**: Regularly analyze wait statistics to identify and resolve resource bottlenecks.

- **Automate Maintenance**: Schedule jobs for index maintenance, statistics updates, and log backups.

11. Monitoring SQL Server with Performance Monitor

Performance Monitor (PerfMon) tracks system and SQL Server-specific metrics. Key SQL Server counters include:

- **SQL Server: Buffer Manager**: Measures memory usage and cache hit ratio.

- **SQL Server: General Statistics**: Tracks user connections and logins.

- **SQL Server: Access Methods**: Monitors table scans, which indicate missing indexes.

- **Physical Disk**: Measures I/O activity, helping you monitor disk performance.

Example of Key Counters:

- **Page Life Expectancy**: Measures the time pages stay in memory; low values may indicate memory pressure.
- **Batch Requests/sec**: Measures the number of batch requests per second, indicating workload levels.
- **Disk Queue Length**: High values indicate disk I/O contention.

Effective monitoring and performance tuning are essential for maintaining a responsive SQL Server environment. This chapter covered monitoring tools like SQL Server Profiler, Extended Events, and DMVs, as well as techniques for query tuning, indexing, memory configuration, and TempDB optimization. By implementing these best practices, you can ensure SQL Server operates efficiently, with minimal downtime and optimal resource utilization. In the next chapter, we'll explore SQL Server high availability and disaster recovery strategies to protect your data and ensure business continuity.